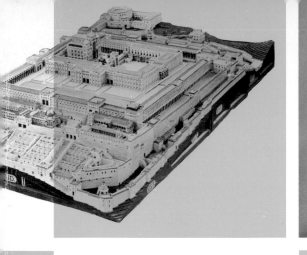

BAKER
STUDIES
IN
BIBLICAL
ARCHAEOLOGY

JeRuSALEM THROUGH the AGES

CHARLES F. PFEIFFER

BAKER STUDIES IN BIBLICAL ARCHAEOLOGY

JERUSALEM
THROUGH THE AGES

BAKER STUDIES IN BIBLICAL ARCHAEOLOGY

JERUSALEM THROUGH THE AGES

by
Charles F. Pfeiffer

BAKER BOOK HOUSE
Grand Rapids, Michigan

Library of Congress Catalog Card Number: 67-18191

49863

PHOTOLITHOPRINTED BY CUSHING - MALLOY, INC.
ANN ARBOR, MICHIGAN, UNITED STATES OF AMERICA
1967

PREFACE

During its long history Jerusalem has been called by many names. Salem, Jebus, Jerusalem, Aelia Capitolina suggest differing political situations. Terms such as the Holy City and the Faithful City (Isa. 1:21) remind us of its spiritual privileges and accomplishments. Yet, in startling metaphor, the prophet dares to apply the names of Sodom and Gomorrah to Jerusalem (Isa. 1:9). The city has mirrored the best, and the worst, of the Jewish, Christian, and Muslim life that has surged through its streets and into its holy places. It was the scene of glorious spiritual revivals under Kings Hezekiah and Josiah, but it also saw the murderous idolatry of an Athaliah and a Manasseh. Many of its people welcomed Jesus as the son of David amid cries of Hosanna. A few days later the cry was, "Crucify him, crucify him!"

The sword has been devouring the people of Jerusalem throughout its checkered career. David took it from the Jebusites, and Nebuchadnezzar took it from the Israelites. During Seleucid times rival factions of Jews vied for control until Antiochus Epiphanes determined to purge the orthodox element. The Maccabees succeeded in gaining their independence, but Rome soon intervened to put down dynastic rivalries and build a larger Roman Empire. The Jews were never satisfied to be ruled by Rome, and the revolts of A.D. 66-70 and A.D. 132-135 decimated the Jews and brought a decisive Roman victory. Rome — later Christianized — was to be humbled by Persians and Arabs. Islam triumphed. The Western world launched a series of crusades, and the streets of Jerusalem flowed with the blood of those whom Christians termed infidels. The crusaders could not gain permanent control of the East, however, and Islam continues to be the dominant faith, with Christians in the minority in the Holy Land. In Old Jerusalem we find devout Muslims at the Dome of the Rock, and devout Christians at the Church of the Holy Sepulchre. The Jew, confined to the western suburbs — Israeli Jerusalem — since 1948, entered the Old City in June, 1967, and prayed at the ancient Wailing Wall. Perhaps no city on earth has known the violence and bloodshed which have characterized the life of Jerusalem through the centuries. Not only in Jeremiah's day did misguided people cry, "Peace, peace," when there was no peace (Jer. 6:14).

It has been the author's aim to give the reader some concept of the continuing history of Jerusalem. Christians are usually aware of the Old Testament and New Testament history of the city, with a few snatches of history from crusader times and an occasional reference in the popular press to contemporary Jerusalem and the Arab-Israeli conflicts. We have tried, within the scope of the *Baker Studies in Biblical Archaeology* series, to present a brief yet perceptive survey of the history of Jerusalem. A bibliography has been appended, and the reader who is interested in studying the history and geography of Jerusalem in greater detail will wish to consult the books listed there.

The author acknowledges with gratitude the assistance given by Mr. Gordon De Young, editor at the Baker Book House. Acknowledgment of the sources of our pictures is given at the appropriate place. Bible quotations are from the Revised Standard Version of the Bible and are given through the courtesy of the Division of Christian Education of the National Council of the Churches of Christ in the U.S.A.

Charles F. Pfeiffer

Central Michigan University
Mt. Pleasant, Michigan
July 1, 1967

CONTENTS

AIR VIEW OF JERUSALEM and its environs. To the right is the Kidron Valley, to the left, the Hinnom Valley. Courtesy, Matson Photo Service

Illustrations

1

JERUSALEM BEFORE DAVID

Jerusalem, a city sacred to the Jew, the Muslim, and the Christian, has been occupied since the fourth millennium B.C. Archaeologists have discovered pottery from that early period which was produced by a people thought to have been Semitic. Occupation continued through the third and early second millennium B.C., although the city of this period was less than nine acres in size.

The first Biblical reference to Jerusalem appears in Genesis 14 where we are told that Abraham, after rescuing Lot and his companions, stopped at a place called Salem, a shortened form of *Yeru-Shalem*, meaning "the foundation of (the god) Shalem." There Abraham met a priest-king with the Semitic name *Melchizedek* ("my king is Zedek") who served as priest to the God *El-Elyon* ("the most high God"). It is significant that at this early period of Biblical history Abraham recognized in Melchizedek a kindred spirit and acknowledged El Elyon as identical with Yahweh (Gen. 14:18-20). Abraham paid tithes to Melchizedek and was blessed by him, acknowledging that Melchizedek was a true priest of God, whether he be named El-Elyon or Yahweh. When the author of the Epistle to the Hebrews sought to prove that Jesus was not only the king of the line of David but also the priest whose sacrifice was superior to those made by the Levitical priests, he insisted that the priesthood of Melchizedek was earlier than and superior to that of the priests who descended from Levi and Aaron (Heb. 7).

Abraham may have come to the vicinity of Jerusalem a second time when he prepared to offer his son Isaac as a sacrifice on a lonely mountain away from the haunts of men in "the land of Moriah" (Gen. 22:2). The term "Moriah" has puzzled Biblical

11

scholars for centuries. The Greek Old Testament known as the Septuagint, dating from the third century B.C., simply reads "the high land" and the Syriac version calls it "the land of the Amorite." The Samaritan tradition removes Moriah completely from the area around Jerusalem and identifies it with Moreh near Shechem. Jewish tradition identifies Moriah with the mountain where Solomon's Temple was later built (cf. II Chron. 3:1). We should remember that the Biblical historian did not see fit to specify in any detail the exact spot where Abraham prepared to offer Isaac, and the most we can say is that it may have been somewhere near, but certainly not in, Melchizedek's Jerusalem.

During the age of the Biblical patriarchs, Jerusalem also appears in the historical records of Egypt. Figurines and pieces of pottery dating from the twentieth century B.C. name Jerusalem and Ashkelon as enemies of Egypt. Among the cuneiform tablets discovered at Tell el-Amarna, Egypt, in 1887 are letters from a king of Jerusalem, named Abdi-Hiba, to the Egyptian Pharaoh Akhenaton. Abdi-Hiba was a vassal of Egypt who reigned during the fourteenth century B.C. when Egyptian power was on the wane in western Asia. Letters imploring aid of Akhenaton were to no avail, although Abdi-Hiba warned that Egyptian aid was

THE KIDRON VALLEY with a monument from the Herodian era to the left, a portion of the wall of Jerusalem at the upper right.

necessary if Egyptian interests were to be maintained in Palestine. Abdi-Hiba's name suggests that he was a Hurrian (or Horite), a member of the non-Semitic people who rose to prominence in Syria, southern Turkey, and parts of Assyria (particularly the Nuzi area) during the sixteenth century B.C. and continued as a major force until the Assyrian conquests of the twelfth century. The Egyptian Merneptah Stele of the thirteenth century B.C. calls the regions of Syria and Palestine where the Israelites were settling *Hurru*, the land of the Hurrians. A strong masonry rampart excavated on the east slope of the Ophel Hill, north of the oldest city of Jerusalem, is of Hurrian origin.

Jerusalem has never had an adequate water supply. Long before David made Jerusalem his stronghold, the Jebusites who occupied the city devised a plan whereby water from the Gihon, a subterranean spring in the Kidron Valley, could be brought into the city. From the spring they dug a horizontal tunnel westward 50 feet into the rock. Then they opened a 40-foot shaft through which water could be drawn up. At the upper end of the shaft was a platform connected with the city by a sloping passage 125 feet long.

At the time of Joshua's conquest of Canaan, Jerusalem was ruled by a king named Adoni-zedek, an Amorite who made an alliance with four other kings in an attempt to prevent Israel from gaining control of southern Canaan. Joshua defeated this confederacy, although Jerusalem was not permanently occupied (Josh. 10). At the division of the land among the tribes, Jerusalem was on the border between Judah and Benjamin (Josh. 15:7-8; 18:16).

The people who dwelt in the city of Jerusalem and the surrounding hill country during the days of Joshua and the judges are termed Jebusites in the Biblical text (Num. 13:29; Josh. 15:8). The Jebusites were a Canaanite tribe (cf. Gen. 10:15), with possible ethnic connections with the Hurrians. Early in the days of the judges, the men of Judah captured Jebusite Jerusalem and burned it (Judg. 1:8). Evidently the Jebusites reoccupied and rebuilt the city (Josh. 15:63; Judg. 1:21), for it was not incorporated into Israelite holdings until the time of David (cf. I Chron. 11:4). Jerusalem is often called Jebus during the period before David, when it was a Jebusite stronghold. The name may have been used by the Hebrews to designate it as the principal city of the Jebusites. Literary evidence makes it clear that Jerusalem, and its shortened form, Salem, were names used for the city almost a millennium before David.

In Jebusite times Israelites seem to have habitually avoided entering Jerusalem. We read of a Levite journeying northward from Bethlehem who arrived in the neighborhood of Jebusite Jerusalem at nightfall. His servant felt that it would be wise to tarry there, but the Levite insisted, ". . . We will not turn aside into the city of foreigners, who do not belong to the people of Israel; but we will pass on to Gibeah" (Judg. 19:10-13). Ironically, in Gibeah the Levite's concubine was abused and died at the hands of those who should have shown hospitality to a sojourner. The Jebusites could not have done worse.

2

DAVID'S JERUSALEM

Two cities are given the title "City of David" in Scripture. Luke tells us that an angel brought good news to shepherds on the hills near Bethlehem, declaring, ". . . to you is born this day in the city of David a Savior, who is Christ the Lord" (Luke 2:11). David was born into the home of Jesse "the Bethlehemite" (I Sam. 16:1), and for that reason he is particularly associated with Bethlehem. The city of Bethlehem, because of its association with the Davidic dynasty, figured in Messianic prophecy. Micah declared, "But you, O Bethlehem Ephrathah, who are little to be among the clans of Judah, from you shall come forth for me one who is to be ruler in Israel, whose origin is from of old, from ancient days" (Micah 5:2).

If Bethlehem was David's city by birth, Jerusalem became David's city by conquest. After the Philistine victory at Mount Gilboa, where Saul and his son Jonathan were slain, David ruled Judah from Hebron (II Sam. 2:1-4) while Saul's son Ishbosheth attempted to rule in dynastic succession over the northern tribes. During the struggle that followed between the north and the south, David increased in power (II Sam. 3:1) and the partisans of Ishbosheth were demoralized to the point where they were ready to desert him. Two of his own captains stole into his bedchamber and beheaded Ishbosheth, thinking that their deed would be rewarded by David (II Sam. 4:1-12). David had the murderers slain, but their deed made it possible for David to claim the allegiance of all Israel (II Sam. 5:1-5).

While Hebron had been a satisfactory capital for the tribe of Judah, a more centrally located city was highly desirable for rule over all Israel. Jerusalem, the Jebusite city on the border of Judah and Benjamin, was ideally situated. Since it had not

15

been incorporated into either tribe it could be conquered and made into royal territory without interfering with existing tribal holdings. Of course, the city first had to be taken from the Jebusites.

Details of the conquest are lacking, but the record makes it clear that the Jebusites were confident that they could defend their city (II Sam. 5:6). David's forces determined that the water supply of Jerusalem was vulnerable. The king challenged his forces to reach the water shaft (II Sam. 5:8), probably to be identified with the ancient rock-cut shaft which was used to convey water from the spring Gihon to the city. Many scholars feel that the city was taken by surprise when the Israelites entered the water shaft. Michel Join-Lambert says:

> A canal system, a Canaanite ṣinnor, led to a source of water in the interior of the city. David made a promise in order to persuade one of his men to volunteer to go up it; Joab, his nephew, the future commander-in-chief of his army, was the first to perform this exploit, to surprize the defenders, and to make success secured.[1]

Attractive as this hypothesis is, more recent scholarship has tended to look for other explanations of the admittedly difficult account of David's victory over the Jebusites (II Sam. 5:6-10). J. Simons suggests that the Israelites knew the location of the strategically important water system which was defended by a strong Jebusite garrison. He says:

> . . . The Israelites were fully acquainted with the location of the spring and . . . with the ṣinnor upon which the life of the city depended. For this reason the Jebusites cannot have neglected to post a guard of warriors at a point somewhere on the slope above the spring in order to prevent the enemy from cutting their life-line. This guard David's most valiant men must "smite" and by doing so "arrive at the ṣinnor" so as to cut the line and force the beleaguered to surrender. The task was a difficult one, as the enemy held a commanding position on the slope, and a very special award was needed to give the necessary impetus to the assault. David held out such a reward and Joab was eager to gain it. With a few select followers he mounted the slope, "smote the Jebusite" and "reached the ṣinnor." From that moment the passage was blocked, the city was doomed, and we are not surprized that the narrator has not thought it worth while to finish his tale, since the order of events was the customary: thirst, despondency, and finally surrender.[2]

---

1 *Jerusalem* (London: 1958), p. 34.
2 *Jerusalem in the Old Testament* (Leiden: 1952), pp. 172 f.

After capturing Jerusalem we read that David "built the city round about from the Millo inward" (II Sam. 5:9). The Millo was probably a tower. The word means a "filling" and it is thought that the tower may have been built over a place where a depression, a ditch, or a breach in the wall was filled in to provide defense for the city. Some archaeologists have dated walls excavated on the southeast hill of Jerusalem to the time of David, but positive identification is lacking. Others suggest that the Millo was to the northwest of Jerusalem, where natural defenses are poor. The answer must await further archaeological work.

The establishment of Jerusalem as capital of the Davidic kingdom had far-reaching historical and religious consequences. Since it had not been part of either the north or the south, Jerusalem provided a neutral spot from which both areas could be governed. As David's personal domain, passed on to his descendants, Jerusalem helped to provide a centralized rallying ground for later generations. When Jerusalem became David's political capital, he determined to make it the religious capital as well. He sent for the ark, which had had no permanent abode since it had fallen into the hands of the Philistines. Amid great festivity, David brought the ark to Jerusalem and placed it inside a specially prepared tent (II Sam. 6:12-19). After he had built a house for himself, with the help of King Hiram of Tyre (II Sam. 5:11), David felt that it would be appropriate to build a suitable house to serve as a sanctuary for Yahweh, Israel's God. The prophet Nathan was at first enthusiastic about the idea, but he later brought a message to David, informing the king that he should not build the "house" but that his son (Solomon) would do so.

We are not certain where David built his palace, but it became the focal point for government in the years after Jerusalem was taken from the Jebusites. Here Nathan rebuked David for his sin with Bathsheba (II Sam. 12:1-6) and here, in David's old age, Absalom usurped the throne while his father had to flee the city (II Sam. 15:16, 35).

Although David did not build the Temple, he did purchase the threshing floor of Araunah the Jebusite on which the Temple was later built. The threshing floor was located north of David's city, presumably outside the walls. The purchase of Araunah's threshing floor and the erection of an altar for burnt offerings and peace offerings (II Sam. 24:25) appear to be the last official acts of David. After a period of senility (I Kings 1:1-4), during

JERUSALEM from the southern slope of the Mount of Olives. The present walls date from the Middle Ages. Courtesy, Matson Photo Service

which time his son Adonijah attempted a coup, David "slept with his fathers and was buried in the city of David" (I Kings 2:10). A traditional "tomb of David" is shown on the southwest hill of Jerusalem but its claims cannot be taken seriously. In David's time the southwest hill was not even a part of Jerusalem, and the tomb itself cannot be earlier than Roman times. Ancient tombs have been excavated on the southeast hill — the Jebusite and Davidic Jerusalem — but identification of David's tomb is impossible today.

3

SOLOMONIC JERUSALEM

Solomon was Israel's first king to have been born in Jerusalem. A child of David and Bath-sheba, he was early chosen to succeed his father. In David's old age another son, Adonijah, attempted to seize the throne and offered the appropriate sacrifices "by the Serpent's Stone which is beside En-rogel" (I Kings 1:9). The term "Serpent's Stone" may represent a stone in the area of En-rogel that was shaped like a serpent or, alternately, a stone which received its name from the fact that it was historically associated with serpent worship. The serpent was a common cult object in ancient Palestine. We read of the "Dragon Well" (K.J.V.) and the "Jackal's Well" (R.S.V.) (Neh. 2:13), and the two words may be related. The Arabs give the name *zahweileh* to a steep and slippery rock slope, and some scholars think I Kings 9 refers to such a place rather than to a serpent. The exact meaning of the term "Stone of Zoheleth" or "Serpent's Stone" is still uncertain.

While Adonijah was working feverishly with his partisans to secure the throne for himself, the prophet Nathan joined Bath-sheba in making a last-minute appeal to David (I Kings 1:11-27). Bath-sheba's son Solomon had been promised the throne, and David ordered that he be anointed at Gihon, east of Jerusalem. Solomon quickly consolidated his power, and the early days of his reign saw Jerusalem at the height of its splendor.

Solomon was the great builder of Jerusalem. He is best known for his Temple, but he also built a palace and fortifications for the city. The Temple had been planned by David, but it was not executed until the time of Solomon. Hiram of Tyre (Ahiram I, *ca.* 968-935 B.C.) provided materials and labor (I Kings 5:1-6) for the project which took seven years to com-

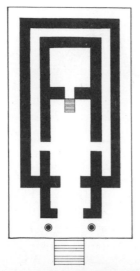

SUGGESTED FLOOR PLAN of the
Temple of Solomon in Jerusalem.

THE HERODIAN TEMPLE AND ITS
ENVIRONS as depicted on a model
by Conrad Shick. Courtesy, Matson
Photo Service

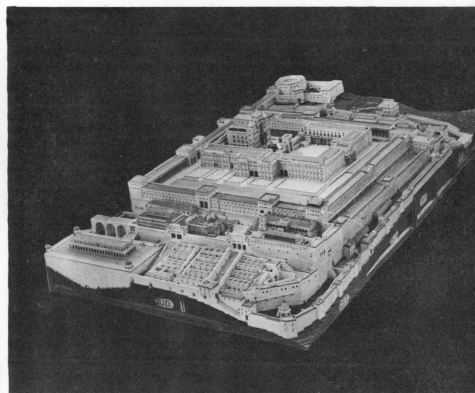

plete (I Kings 6:38). Forced labor battalions were assigned to work in the forests of Lebanon and in the Judean quarries to provide material for the Temple (I Kings 5:13-18).

The threshing floor which David had purchased from Araunah was without doubt leveled off and enclosed within walls to make a sacred area, comparable to the area enclosed for Muslim worship around the Dome of the Rock today. The Temple itself was a comparatively simple structure. Its interior measurements formed an oblong 60 cubits long by 20 cubits wide (about 100 feet by 30 feet). It was 30 cubits high.

At the front of the Temple was a porch or vestibule, 10 cubits deep and 20 cubits wide. Beyond the porch was the "holy place," 40 cubits long. Finally there was the "holy of holies" or "most holy place" in the form of a cube measuring 20 cubits in each dimension. Side rooms or chambers surrounded the Temple except for the porch.

In front of the porch were two bronze pillars (I Kings 7:15) which were given the names Jachin and Boaz (II Chron. 3: 15-17). R. B. Y. Scott has suggested that these names are the first words of longer inscriptions. Jachin may represent: "He will establish (yakin) the throne of David forever." Boaz could represent "In the strength of (beoz) Yahweh shall the king rejoice."[1]

The pillars were about 31 feet high, about 6½ feet in diameter, and hollow. The metal of the pillars was about 3 inches thick. Structurally they were independent of the Temple porch, standing free in front of it. W. F. Albright has held that they served as huge cressets, or fire altars, in which the suet of the sacrifices was burned.[2]

Passing between the pillars we reach the porch or vestibule, 20 cubits wide and 10 cubits deep. Beyond was the Temple proper, a room 40 cubits long with an altar at the far end, in front of the entrance to the inner sanctuary, known as the Holy of Holies, or the Most Holy Place. In the Holy of Holies was the sacred ark which served as the repository for the two tablets of the Law (Exod. 25:16, 21; 40:20). The ark was a rectangular box, 2½ by 1½ by 1½ cubits. It was made of acacia wood, overlaid

---

1 R. B. Y. Scott, "The Pillars Jachin and Boaz," *JBL* LVIII (1939), pp. 143f.

2 The view was first propounded by W. Robertson Smith in his *Religion of the Semites* (Baltimore: 1894), pp. 487-490. Albright presents more recent archaeological evidence in his *Archaeology and the Religion of Israel* (1942), pp. 144-148.

with gold. On the lid of the ark were two golden cherubim, each 10 cubits high and with wings outspread.

At the center of the Muslim sacred enclosure called the Haram-es-Sherif ("the noble sanctuary") in the Old City of Jerusalem, below the Dome of the Rock (the so-called "Mosque of Omar") is a large boulder which has been venerated since ancient times. This may well be the place where David built an altar and where the Holy of Holies of Solomon's Temple stood.

The Temple became the center of religious life for Israel during the years that followed its dedication. With the division

THE ROCK around which the Moslem Dome of the Rock was built. The Holy of Holies of the Solomonic Temple is believed to have been built over this rock.

of the kingdom, the northern tribes built sanctuaries at Bethel and Dan, but the Temple and the Davidic dynasty remained the religious and political foci for the life of Judah.

Solomon built, in addition to the Temple, an ornate palace for himself. This included "the House of the Forest of Lebanon," with forty-five columns hewn from the trunks of cedars and placed in three rows. This room, 180 feet long and 50 feet high, served as a reception hall. Adjoining it was a smaller vestibule, beyond which was the Throne Room. There at the top of six steps, each flanked by two lions, was the king's ivory throne. The palace proper was evidently spacious, for there Solomon maintained his harem of seven hundred wives and three hundred concubines.

The fortification and defense of Jerusalem was another responsibility of Solomon. He fortified an area known as the Millo, probably a fortress in the exposed northwestern sector of the city, which was vulnerable to attack. Solomon also is credited with building "the wall around Jerusalem" (I Kings 3:1; 9:15). The building of the Temple required an extension of the earlier walls.

Solomon's wisdom, his wealth, and the grandeur of his court became proverbial. Jerusalem became a cosmopolitan center into which came the tribute of subject peoples and emissaries of the people themselves. Solomon's wives represented many nations and many religions. The king felt obligated to cater to their tastes, with the result that temples to those gods began to appear in the environs of the Holy City. A hill above the village of Siloam is known today as the Mount of Offense because of the tradition that idolatrous shrines were built there by Solomon.

There is irony in the fact that the wise Solomon allowed his wives to alienate him from Yahweh. That alienation brought political and economic problems to the last years of Solomon's reign. Subject peoples began to reject Solomon's claims upon them. The Arameans of Damascus arose as an independent nation. Egypt showed sufficient lack of friendship to welcome Jeroboam, a disaffected official who fled from Solomon.

With the absence of tribute, the tax burden for the Israelites became enormous, and the people were drafted into forced labor battalions. Resentment grew, but Solomon did not live to see the open break with the Davidic dynasty.

4

DIVISION AND RESTORATION

The forced labor and the high tax burdens imposed by Solomon proved more than his kingdom could bear. While the actual division of the kingdom did not take place until after Solomon's death, there can be no doubt that the king's fiscal policies were making division inevitable. When Solomon's son Rehoboam attempted to take the throne, the northern tribes rebelled. Jerusalem, once the fairly central capital of united Israel, became the capital of the small kingdom of Judah which included the tribes of Judah and Benjamin. The northern kingdom, called Israel, was larger, wealthier, and more exposed to foreign influences than was Judah. Samaria, which became the capital of Israel, outranked Jerusalem in its wealth and beauty. Jerusalem, however, continued to be the religious center of Yahweh-worship in the south. The loyalty of the southern kingdom to the Davidic dynasty gave it a more stable government than the north was to enjoy with its succession of kings, some weak and some strong.

Jerusalem suffered a period of decline during the first century after the division of the kingdom. The northern kingdom threatened Judah's northern borders, and the invasion of Sheshonq I (Biblical Shishak) of Egypt brought a threat from the south. The Egyptians were able to take advantage of the weakness of Judah and Israel following their separation to press ancient claims on the territories of western Asia. As the Egyptian army entered the environs of Jerusalem, Rehoboam bought him off with palace and Temple treasures.

Recovery took place during the years from the reign of Jehoshaphat (871-849 B.C.) to Joash (837-789 B.C.). Jehoshaphat enlarged Jerusalem by building a new square on the eastern

24

side of the city. Israel and Judah adopted a policy of peaceful co-existence and both enjoyed a period of renewed prestige. When Athaliah, daughter of the infamous Ahab and Jezebel of the Omri dynasty in Israel, seized the throne of Judah, she attempted to introduce Baalism as the state religion. She laid waste the Temple and subsidized her Baalist priesthood. The priests of Yahweh were successful in protecting an infant boy of the Davidic line from the wrath of Athaliah, and ultimately in proclaiming him king. The High Priest Jehoiada served as regent and adviser to the boy, Joash, until he was old enough to assume power in his own right. This marks the beginning of priestly activity in the political life of Judah. Joash restored the desecrated Temple and collected funds for its upkeep.

Jerusalem suffered humiliation again when Jehoash of Israel defeated Amaziah of Judah (798-784 B.C.) and breached the walls of Jerusalem from the Gate of Ephraim to the Corner Gate (II Kings 14:13). Riches from the palace and the Temple were carried off to Samaria. During the reign of Uzziah, however, Judah became strong and prosperous again. Uzziah built towers at the Corner Gate and the Valley Gate of Jerusalem and fortified them with "engines made by cunning men, to be upon the towers and upon the bulwarks, to shoot arrows and great stones withal" (II Chron. 26:9, 15). A royal palace and fortress discovered at Ramat Rahel, three miles south of Biblical Jerusalem, may date from the time of Uzziah.

During the reign of Ahaz, Jerusalem was threatened by a coalition of the kings of Israel and the Aramean kingdom of Damascus who were prepared to resist the growing power of Assyria. Ahaz of Judah was unwilling to join them with the result that they decided to remove him from the throne and place a puppet ruler, Ben-Tabeel, in Jerusalem. Isaiah the prophet assured the weak Ahaz that Yahweh would not permit the Davidic throne to be taken from him and that both Syria and Israel would fall before Assyria (Isa. 7).

In 722 B.C. Samaria fell. The kingdom of Judah had no need of fear from Samaria or from Damascus, which had fallen a decade earlier, but the Assyrian himself would pose a still greater threat. To prepare for possible siege, King Hezekiah prepared to augment the water supply of Jerusalem. Previously cisterns which collected rain water were the only source of water within the walled city. Outside, in the Kidron Valley, were the waters of the Gihon. Hezekiah determined to bring the water from the Gihon into the city and to hide the spring from any potential

THE POOL OF SILOAM, a source of water for the people of Jerusalem. Water was brought to it through the Siloam Tunnel from the Gihon Spring, in the Kidron Valley. Courtesy, Matson Photo Service

THE SILOAM TUNNEL, built in the time of Hezekiah to bring water from the Gihon Spring in the Kidron Valley to the city of Jerusalem. Courtesy, Matson Photo service

enemy. The Biblical historian says, "[Hezekiah] made a pool and a conduit, and brought water into the city" (II Kings 20:20). The chronicler says, "He took counsel with his princes and his mighty men to stop the waters of the fountains which were without the city" (II Chron. 32:30).

The tunnel dug by Hezekiah's men to conduct water from the Gihon spring to the Pool of Siloam, inside the city, is still in use. In 1880 an inscription dating from Hezekiah's time was discovered just inside the opening within the city. It tells how two teams of men started to dig out the tunnel, one from each end. They made contact by means of sound, joining one another to complete the eighteen-hundred-foot tunnel. The tunnel is a remarkable engineering feat for its time, and the inscription is one of our earliest examples of Hebrew writing.

That Hezekiah's preparations were needed was demonstrated during the invasion of Judah, and siege of Jerusalem by Sennacherib of Assyria in 701 B.C. Judah fell prostrate before the conqueror, but Jerusalem alone stood in defiance. The annals of Sennacherib suggest that Hezekiah was a leader of the opposition to Sennacherib in western Asia. The Biblical and Assyrian records agree that Sennacherib did not enter Jerusalem, and that he did lift his siege after receiving tribute. The Assyrian Annals state:

> As for Hezekiah the Jew, who did not submit to my yoke, 46 of his strong walled cities, as well as the small cities in their neighborhood, which were without number, — by leveling with battering rams [?] and by bringing up siege-engines [?], by attacking, and storming on foot, by mines, tunnels, and breaches [?], I besieged and took [those cities]. 200,150 people, great and small, male and female, horses, mules, asses, camels, cattle and sheep

without number, I brought away from them and counted as spoil. Himself, like a caged bird, I shut up in Jerusalem, his royal city. Earthworks I threw up against him, — the one coming out of the city gate I turned back to his misery. The cities of his which I had despoiled, I cut off from his land, and I gave [them] to Mitinti, king of Ashdod, Padi, king of Ekron, and Silli-bel, king of Gaza. And [thus] I diminished his land. I added to the former tribute, and laid upon him the giving up of their land [as well as] imposts — gifts for my majesty. As for Hezekiah, the terrifying splendor of my majesty overcame him, and the Urbi [Arabs] and his mercenary [?] troops which he had brought in to strengthen Jerusalem, his royal city, deserted him. In addition to the 30 talents of gold and 800 talents of silver, [there were] gems, antimony, jewels [?], large *sandu*-stones, couches of ivory, house-chairs of ivory, elephant hide, ivory [lit., "elephant's teeth"], ebony [?], boxwood [?], all kinds of valuable [heavy] treasures, as well as his daughters, his harem, his male and female musicians, which he had [them] bring after me to Nineveh, my royal city. To pay tribute and to accept [lit., do] servitude, he dispatched his messengers.

While the annals give no hint of the destruction of Sennacherib's army (II Kings 19:35-37), they do make it clear that Sennacherib had to be content with his booty, and that Jerusalem was spared. The Assyrians went home, perhaps as a result of an epidemic which the Israelites interpreted as a sign of divine deliverance.

Had Sennacherib succeeded in destroying Jerusalem and taking its populace into exile, as Sargon did at the destruction of Samaria (722 B.C.), there would have been no return. The Assyrians transported populations, scattering their former enemies to prevent them from reuniting. This policy resulted in the so-called "lost tribes" of the north, which never returned as a people. Remnants of them made their way south at the time of the fall of Samaria, and others doubtless came at other times, but the continuity of Israelite history was ended at the time of their deportation. Continuity was not lost in the south, for the kingdom of Judah maintained its independence until after the fall of Nineveh (612 B.C.).

King Hezekiah had been a loyal Yahwist, but his successors, Manasseh and Amon, reverted to idolatry. The old Baal worship was revived and new cults were introduced from Assyria. Children were offered in sacrifice to the god Molech in the Valley of Hinnom. Prophets denounced Judah and its rulers for faithlessness to their covenant with Yahweh, but the warnings went unheeded (cf. Ezek. 8:10-14).

King Josiah reversed the policy of Manasseh and Amon and
sought to bring Judah back to Yahweh and his law. Assyrian
power had been successfully challenged by Nabopolazzar of
Babylon, and Judah had a brief breathing spell before Babylon
would seek to incorporate her into a new empire. After cleansing and renovating the Temple and vowing fidelity to Yahweh's
Law, Josiah was killed at Megiddo in battle with Pharaoh Neco's
Egyptian army. Egypt at long last had ceased her quarrel with
Assyria and was going to join the remnants of the Assyrian army
to check the Babylonian forces of Nebuchadnezzar, Nabopolazzar's son. Josiah, who may have had a treaty with the Babylonians, tried to stop the Egyptians from marching through his
territory. The result was fatal for Josiah, but he may have
delayed the Egyptians long enough to prevent their joining the
Assyrians. Nebuchadnezzar moved on through Syria into Palestine. In 605 B.C. he defeated Neco at Carchemish on the
Euphrates and in 598 B.C. he besieged Jerusalem. The king,
Jehoiachin, was exiled to Babylon along with the leading government officials and representatives of the city's elite. The
prophet Jeremiah warned Jehoiachin's uncle and successor.
Zedekiah, that further revolt would be tragic, but Egypt offered
aid and Judah again rebelled against Nebuchadnezzar. In 587
B.C. the army of Nebuchadnezzar again besieged Jerusalem and
this time the Babylonians would not content themselves with
captives and booty. After the northern wall was breached the
Babylonians entered the city, seized what they desired, and
then burned both the palace and the Temple. The Babylonian
Chronicle reads:

> In the seventh year [of Nebuchadnezzar], in the month of Kislev,
> the Babylonian king mustered his troops and, having marched to
> the land of Hatti [i.e., Syria-Palestine], beseiged the city of Judah
> [i.e., Jerusalem]. On the second day of the month Adar he cap-
> tured the city and seized the king. He set up in it a king after
> his heart and, having received its heavy tribute, sent them [i.e., the
> Judeans] to Babylon.

Zedekiah attempted an escape but he was captured, taken to
Nebuchadnezzar's camp and forced to see his children slain
before his eyes. Then Zedekiah was blinded and taken to
Babylon (II Kings 24:10-17). An attempt was made to rule the
remnants of the Jews through a governor named Gedaliah, appointed by the Babylonians. He was slain by a group of extremists and Judea was reduced to a waste. Only the "poor of

the land" were left in Judah (II Kings 25:12). The Babylonians did not repopulate Jerusalem, as the Assyrians had done to Samaria, and the exiles in Babylon, encouraged by Ezekiel, looked forward to the day when they would return to Zion and build a new Temple to Yahweh.

While many Jews prospered in Babylon, the faithful remnant longed for the day of deliverance from exile and return to the Holy City. Deliverance came in the person of Cyrus of Anshan, founder of the Persian Empire whose conquest of Babylon in 536 B.C. ushered in a new era for the Jews. Cyrus issued a decree permitting Jews to return to Jerusalem to rebuild the Temple to their God Yahweh. This decree was in accord with the policy of Cyrus to court the favor of subject peoples by allowing them to rebuild their shrines and to return to their homelands. In the Cyrus Cylinder, Cyrus said:

> . . . I returned to [these] sacred cities on the other side of the Tigris, the sanctuaries of which have been ruins for a long time, the images which [used] to live therein and established for them permanent sanctuaries. I also gathered all their [former] inhabitants and returned [to them] their habitations. Furthermore, I resettled upon the command of Marduk, the great lord, all the gods of Sumer and Akkad whom Nabonidus has brought into Babylon to the anger of the lord of the gods, unharmed, in their [former] chapels, the places which make them happy.

Cyrus thus posed as a deliverer. Subject peoples had their gods and their lands restored. Cyrus might well have felt the need of having loyal subjects in Palestine, for he had designs on Egypt and would need a strong, loyal buffer state.

A small company of Jews began the trek from Babylon to Jerusalem with the blessing and support of Cyrus. We read of a prince of the line of Judah named Sheshbazzar who was named governor of Judah. Sheshbazzar laid the foundation of the Temple and reestablished the sacrificial worship (Ezra 1:8, 11; 5:14, 16). We read also of Zerubbabel, whom some scholars equate with Sheshbazzar, and a High Priest named Jeshua, son of Jozadak, who were leaders of the Jews who returned to Jerusalem. Judea was subject to the Persian Empire, and Persia found it expedient to hold the High Priests accountable for internal Jewish affairs. In this way the priesthood became politically involved. While devout Jews looked for a king of the Davidic line to restore their political sovereignty at a future time, for the present the priesthood combined functions of church and state.

Ezra "the scribe" was another leader who brought Jews from Babylon to Jerusalem. His very office is expressive of the devotion to law — Hebrew Torah — which characterized pious Jews during and after the Exile. Scribes were more than copyists. They studied and taught the law, interpreting it and applying it to the divergent circumstances of Israelite life.

The lay counterpart to Ezra was Nehemiah, an officer in the Persian court, who obtained a leave of absence to help his Jewish compatriots in Jerusalem. In 440 B.C. Nehemiah was appointed governor of Jerusalem. His principal challenge was the rebuilding of the walls of Jerusalem, which had been in ruins since the days of Nebuchadnezzar. The spirit of self-sacrifice and the enthusiasm for the task which he exhibited were enough to spur the people on, and within fifty-two days the wall was completed (Neh. 6:15-18).

Nehemiah has given us a description of his tour of inspection (Neh. 2:11-16); it is our best description of the extent of the city at the time of the return from exile. To the east the city walls paralleled the Kidron. They then encircled the Ophel Mount and crossed the Tyropoeon valley below Siloam. The walls continued, climbing up the western hill, possibly to the site of the present Jaffa Gate, and then turned eastward, linking up with the Temple enclosure.

The building of the Temple and the wall excited the jealousy and antagonism of the Samaritans and other "adversaries of Judah and Benjamin" who had profited by the absence of the Jews from Jerusalem. They resented the efforts of those who sought to reconstitute Jewish life, and tried every diplomatic and political maneuver that they could devise to delay the work of reconstruction. On the other hand, prophets such as Haggai and Zechariah encouraged the Jews to finish the house of Yahweh, with the assurance that its glory would exceed that of the Temple built by Solomon. Actually the Second Temple was much humbler than that of Solomon, built early in his reign when Israel was a major power with tribute flowing into its capital. The Second Temple was built at a time when the Jews were a subject people. Their prophetic leaders, however, assured them that God would restore Israel to a position of greatness, and that a Davidic king would rule in justice from Jerusalem, bringing blessing to the ends of the earth. Such hopes would sustain

Israel in the trials she was to face in the years following her return from Babylon.

Ezra and Nehemiah were particularly concerned that the Jews be a holy people. Among the problems they faced was the inter-marriage of Jews with their non-Jewish neighbors. Recalling that even Solomon was led astray by his idolatrous wives, Ezra and Nehemiah sought to purge Jerusalem of this source of potential danger.

The Jews in Jerusalem enjoyed comparative prosperity in the years that followed the careers of Ezra and Nehemiah. High Priests were concerned that the city be ruled well, and learned scribes gave attention to interpreting the law. Some Jews found places of service outside Jerusalem, for the Persians found them highly trustworthy public servants. To the orthodox, however, Jerusalem was still the center of their affection and their religious devotion.

5

THE HELLENISTIC CITY

In 334 B.C. Alexander, son of Philip of Macedon, moved his armies eastward and began his march through Asia Minor, then down the Palestinian coast into Egypt. His goal was the conquest of the Persian Empire and the incorporation of its vast territories into his own. The legend that he visited Jerusalem cannot be taken seriously, but the fact that his conquests had profound influences on Jewish life must be recognized. The Babylonian Exile had taught the Jews the folly of idolatry. From her entrance into Canaan until her captivity in Babylon, Israel had been sorely tempted to follow the Canaanite fertility cult and forget her covenant to serve Yahweh alone. One important consequence of the Exile was the lesson that Yahwism must not be diluted with any form of paganism.

The Jews who returned from Babylon were prepared to live their lives in religious isolation. They felt no need of help from the Samaritans in building their Temple, and they certainly felt no need to learn the art of living from Alexander and his successors. Jews were welcome in Alexandria and other Hellenistic cities. As a well-disciplined, moral people they were admired by the Hellenists as they had been admired by the Persians. Jews in Egypt often adopted Greek habits, Greek dress, Greek names, and even a Greek philosophy. Yet the Jews of Palestine, and of Jerusalem in particular, tended to be more conservative in their approach.

As long as the Ptolemies of Egypt controlled Palestine, the Jews had nothing to fear. Some of the young might adopt Greek ways, but the religion of the fathers could be practiced freely and Jewish religion and culture were genuinely respected.

The Hebrew Scriptures had been translated into Greek in Alexandria.

When, in 198 B.C., Antiochus III of Syria defeated the Egyptians at Paneas, near one of the sources of the Jordan, the situation changed radically. The Syrian Seleucids dreamed of unifying Asia on the basis of a Hellenistic civilization. Not only did they encourage Greek architecture and language, along with Greek dress and philosophy, but Greek religious ideals and modes of daily life were prescribed for all their peoples.

Some Jews were convinced that their future rested in conformity to the new Hellenistic approach. Others saw Hellenism as a new challenge to their ancestral faith. Before Hellenism became a real threat from without, it had gained a considerable following within the fold of Judaism. The Hellenistic faction had its opportunity when, in 175 B.C., Antiochus IV ("Epiphanes") became king and sought to bring Jerusalem into conformity with his Hellenistic policy. A gymnasium was erected in Jerusalem and Greek customs were introduced. While many objected, Antiochus might have succeeded in making some changes in Jewish life, had he not made the mistake of striking at the Temple itself. Antiochus installed a Syrian garrison in Jerusalem and built a fortress, the Akra, to control the city. He then abolished the worship of Yahweh from the Temple and installed a statue of the Olympian Zeus as the object of worship.

The revolt against Antiochus did not begin in Jerusalem but in Modin, a small settlement to the northwest. There an aged priest named Mattathias refused to obey the command of Antiochus' emissary. Instead of offering the prescribed heathen sacrifice, Mattathias killed the emissary, along with an apostate Jew who was prepared to deny his faith. With his sons, Mattathias escaped to the Judean hill country and prepared to wage guerilla war on the Syrians.

The word of Mattathias' brave response to Syrian tyranny spread throughout Judea, and thousands of young men joined the forces of revolt. Soon after the war began, Mattathias died, but he was succeeded by the brave Judas (or Judah) who was surnamed Maccabaeus ("the hammer"). Judas wisely determined to gain control of the countryside before attacking Jerusalem itself. Lysias, viceroy to Antiochus, prepared to march an army southward to put down the revolt when he received word that Antiochus Epiphanes had died. Lysias determined to consolidate his own strength in Syria rather than to dissipate it in a war with the Jews. A truce was declared, and the city of

Jerusalem was divided. The Jews were permitted to rebuild
their Temple and to reinstitute 'Temple sacrifices. The Syrian
garrison occupied the Akra and policed the city, with orders not
to molest the Jews.

Judas and those associated with him began the task of cleans-
ing the Temple and preparing it for the worship of Yahweh.
They pulled down the altar to Zeus and set up an altar to
Yahweh. On the twenty-fifth day of Kislev (December), 165
B.C. — exactly three years after its profanation — the Temple
lamps were lit again. The Jewish festival of Hanukkah, the
Feast of Lights, celebrates the cleansing of the Temple after the
victory of the Maccabees.

While the religious party of the *Hasidim* ("the pious"), those
anti-Hellenistic Jews that supported Judas in his attempt to restore a pure Yahwism to Israel, were satisfied with the assurance
of religious freedom, Judas himself felt he should press on to
achieve political freedom as well. At his death he was succeeded
by a brother, Jonathan, and he, in turn, by another brother,
Simon. Jonathan was given the office of High Priest and Governor of Judah, suggesting the Maccabean claim to full sovereignty.
In 141 B.C. Simon succeeded in taking the Akra, with the result
that Jerusalem became wholly Jewish until its destruction by
Titus in A.D. 70. Simon's line was honored with the position
of hereditary high priest. In 135 B.C. he was succeeded by his
son John Hyrcanus who succeeded in building a Jewish nation
on the foundations of the Maccabean state. Rome was a growing
power in the East, and Rome was content to allow Hyrcanus
full sway in southern Palestine as a check on the Syrian kingdom
in the north. Rome showed its friendship to Hyrcanus by
passing a senatorial decree demanding that Syria renounce all
claim to the Jews and their territory, and ordering Syria to
recognize the independence of Judea as an ally of Rome.

The successes of Hyrcanus brought their own problems. His
armies incorporated Idumea to the south and Samaria to the
north into the Jewish state. The Samaritan temple on Mount
Gerizim was razed in an act of vengeance for past wrongs, but
the result was to perpetuate the feud between Jew and Samaritan. Hyrcanus began with all the spiritual ideals of the earlier
Hasidim and their successors, the Pharisees. The lust for power,
however, brought changes over Hyrcanus. Before his death he
broke with the Pharisees and sided with the pro-Hellenistic
Sadducees. The rule of the Maccabees had reached its zenith.

Hyrcanus was succeeded by his energetic son Aristobulus who

added Galilee to the Jewish state and forcibly converted its people to Judaism. The Jerusalem Jews looked down on the Galileans. The taunt, "Can any good thing come out of Nazareth?" expresses the feeling. Aristobulus died within a year of his taking the throne, but his brother Alexander Jannaeus (103-76 B.C.) was no improvement. Jannaeus was Hellenistic in his sympathies and he scorned the orthodox faith of the Pharisees. When they showed their anger by flinging lemons at him, chasing him out of the Temple, he ordered a massacre and it is said that six thousand Pharisees were slain at the king's command. Thus the party of the Pharisees became the sworn enemy of the Maccabean rulers.

When Jannaeus' widow, Salome Alexandra, succeeded him, the religious policy was reversed. Pharisees returned from exile and, with the queen's cooperation, they turned their wrath on the Sadducees. The result was a sparring for advantage. Salome's son Hyrcanus (II) was High Priest during his mother's reign, but the Sadducees backed another son, Aristobulus (II) and offered their aid to help him unseat his mother and his brother. When Salome Alexandra died, civil war was imminent.

Aristobulus, supported by the Sadducees, seized Jerusalem and his brother Hyrcanus fled. An Idumaean prince, Antipater, arranged for Hyrcanus to be protected in Petra while plans were made for the reconquest of Jerusalem. A new factor was added, however, when Scaurus, a lieutenant in the service of Pompey, appeared on the scene. Scaurus decided to accept the status quo, allowing Aristobulus to keep Jerusalem, until Pompey could visit Jerusalem.

In 63 B.C. Pompey decided to disband the Jewish monarchy and add Judea to the Roman province of Syria. Aristobulus foolishly decided to fight the Romans in order to hold his kingdom. Antipater proved helpful to the Romans by working with the Pharisees to keep the countryside peaceful and cooperative. In the end the Romans dislodged Aristobulus, sending him and his children to Rome as prisoners. Hyrcanus was installed High Priest of the Jews, and Antipater served as the real power in the political arena.

6

NEW TESTAMENT JERUSALEM

With the conquests of Pompey in 63 B.C. Jerusalem was made subject to Rome. Pompey, Tacitus tells us, entered the very Holy of Holies of the Temple, and was surprised to find it empty. The Greeks and Romans placed colossal statues of their gods in their temples, but the Israelite Temple was empty.

The efficient Romans placed Judea under Scaurus, Propraeter of Syria. Taxes were heavy, but Judea was given a large amount of autonomy. An Idumaean — i.e., a descendant of the Old Testament Edomites — named Antipater was able to gain considerable power in Judea as a result of his clever politicking. He had supported Pompey until, during the Civil War, he found it expedient to back Julius Caesar. Caesar was assassinated in 44 B.C. and Antipater died of poison in 43 B.C. Yet Antipater had been so politically astute that his sons Herod and Phasael became tetrarchs of Judea in 41 B.C.

COIN OF HEROD THE GREAT. Courtesy, British Museum

SITE OF THE TOWER OF ANTONIA at the northwest corner of the Temple area. Courtesy, Matson Photo Service

When the Parthians invaded Palestine the Jews hailed them as liberators. Herod espoused the cause of Rome and went into exile. The Romans rewarded him by naming him king of the province of Judea. When, in 38 B.C., the Romans drove the Parthians out, Herod came back with two Roman legions to claim his territory. To make his rule legitimate in Jewish eyes, Herod married Mariamne, a descendant of the Hasmoneans. The Jews never ceased to regard him as a hated foreigner, but he had the support of Rome and reigned from 37 B.C. to 4 B.C.

Herod ruled during prosperous times, and even Jewish resentment against the hated Idumaean could not diminish the glory Herod acquired through his building projects. As a result of the peace which the Augustan Age brought to the Roman world, Jewish pilgrims made their way to the Holy City in large numbers. They, and their fellow Jews who did not travel, made large contributions to the Temple. As an efficient tax collector, Herod was able to bring additional funds into Jerusalem in order to beautify and, if necessary, to defend it.

At the northwestern corner of the Temple Mount, on the site of the Hasmonean Fortress Baris, Herod built the Fortress Antonia, named after Mark Antony. The Antonia was built in the form of a massive square, with four strong towers. Two water cisterns were under the paving slabs of the interior court. The Fortress could be entered from the street through a double arch-

MODEL OF THE FORTRESS OF ANTONIA, Roman military headquarters in New Testament times. Courtesy, Ecce Homo Orphanage

way. Direct access was possible from the Antonia into the court of the Temple. The garrison maintained in the fortress could control the Temple area when necessary.

Excavations under the monastery of the Sisters of Sion have brought to light a portion of the pavement of the Antonia court. Carved on some of the stones are markings for games used by the Roman soldiers in passing their leisure hours. The cisterns are still intact and they receive the winter rains now as they did two millennia ago. The excavators discovered stone bullets which were used during the siege of A.D. 70.

Herod's second fortress was at the western extremity of Jerusalem at the site of the Royal Palace. This building, begun in 24 B.C., had three towers named Phasael, for Herod's brother; Hippicus, for a friend; and Mariamne, for his wife. The stump of Phasael, the largest tower, still stands as part of the so-called Tower of David.

In a vain attempt to conciliate his Jewish subjects, Herod reconstructed their Temple on a grand style. Herod was careful

GREEK INSCRIPTION which forbade Gentiles to enter the court of the Jews in the Herodian Temple. "Let no stranger penetrate beyond the barrier and the peribola that enclose the sanctuary. Whoever may be caught attempting to do so will have only himself to blame if his death should ensue in consequence." Courtesy, The Louvre

THE JEWISH WAILING WALL. For centuries devout Jews have come to the "Wailing Wall" to mourn and to pray for the restoration of Jerusalem.

not to do anything that might be contrary to Jewish law. He taught a thousand priests the building trade so they might work on the Holy of Holies, where non-priests had no right to enter. The construction was begun in 20 B.C., and it was not finished until A.D. 64, just six years before the armies of Titus destroyed both city and Temple.

Even the Jewish rabbis extolled the beauty of Herod's Temple: "He who has not beheld the Temple of Herod has never seen beauty in his life."[1] The architecture accorded with the best of Hellenistic-Roman times. It occupied an enclosure 2,575 feet by 985 feet, to which access might be gained through eight gates. The Temple itself had two concentric courts: an outer "Court of the Gentiles" to which non-Jews were admitted, and the interior court for the Jews. Two stone inscriptions warning Gentiles not to enter the inner court, under pain of death, have been discovered. The inner court was further divided into three parts: one for women, one for men, and a court in front of the sanctuary reserved for the priests and Levites.

Fourteen steps led up to the Temple itself, designed after that

---

1 Talmud Tractate *Baba Batra,* 3b.

THE LITHOSTROTOS. The pavement of the Court of Antonia was known as the Lithostrotos. The huge paving stones are Herodian. Pilate's judgment of Jesus may have taken place here.

of Solomon. Its facade of marble and gold is said to have appeared in the distance as a "mountain of snow glittering in the sun." The sanctuary proper, 65 feet long, was separated from the Holy of Holies by a curtain. No expense was spared. The gateway was surmounted with a vine of gold, symbolic of Israel. Golden needles were used to prevent birds from soiling the roof.

Some examples of Herodian architecture and masonry survive today. The "Wailing Wall," so named because Jews came for centuries to mourn there and to pray for the restoration of their city, is actually part of the western wall of the Temple court. The tombs of the Herodian family have been identified along with numerous other tombs of the period. The so-called Tomb of Absalom in the Kidron Valley is thought to date from Herodian times.

For nine years after Herod's death his inept son Archelaus (4 B.C.—A.D. 6) ruled Palestine. From A.D. 6 to 41, and from A.D. 44 to 66, Judea was governed by a succession of procurators, the fifth of whom was Pontius Pilate (A.D. 26-36). Apart from the visit of Jesus to Jerusalem with Mary and Joseph, in his childhood (Luke 2:41-51), all of the associations of Jesus with Jerusalem were during Pilate's procuratorship.

CARVINGS ON THE LITHOSTROTOS. The "King's Game," played with dice, occupied the time of soldiers stationed in the Antonia.

While Jesus, like David before him, had been born in Bethlehem, it was in Jerusalem and its environs that his life reached its tragic climax. The Bethany home of Mary, Martha, and Lazarus was east of the city. From Bethany Jesus passed through a gate in the eastern wall of Jerusalem to make his triumphal entry as the people waved their palm branches and shouted, "Hosanna." Jesus ministered in the city beneath the portico of the Temple, but evenings found him in the Bethany home. Knowing his hour was soon to come, Jesus sent his disciples ahead on Thursday evening to prepare for the Passover. Tradition points to the Coenaculum on Mt. Zion as the spot. There Jesus instituted the Communion, announcing his impending death. From the room in which the Last Supper was observed, Jesus and his disciples retired into Gethsemane (*Gat-shemanim*, "Oil press"). Gethsemane must have been at or near the site pointed out today and maintained by the Franciscans. Olive trees have grown in this area from ancient times to the present. There Jesus was arrested and taken by the Captain of the Temple to the house of the High Priest Caiaphas, placed by tradition a short distance from the Coenaculum. Jesus was interrogated there and declared to be guilty of blasphemy and subject to the death penalty. Since the Jewish rabbinical court known as the Sanhedrin did not have the authority to pronounce capital punishment, Jesus was turned over to Pontius Pilate who was in the city at the time to prevent possible disturbances during the Passover season.

Tradition states that Pilate was at the Fortress Antonia at the time that Jesus was brought to him, that it was at the Ecce Homo arch that Jesus was exhibited to the people before the crucifixion ("Behold the Man," John 19:5), and that it was the stone pavement of the Antonia Court — the Lithostrotos — where Jesus was judged. Pilate then sent Jesus to the Tetrarch Herod, whose house was close to where the Upper City joined the Temple Mount at the site of "Wilson's Arch." Herod sent Jesus back to Pilate, who condemned him as a political offender who had accepted the title "King of the Jews."

The place of the crucifixion and of Joseph's tomb has been identified since the time of Constantine (A.D. 335) with a church known to the Greeks as the Anastasis ("Resurrection") and to the Latins as the Church of the Holy Sepulchre. The church is inside the present Old City of Jerusalem, within the

THE GARDEN TOMB, believed by some to be the tomb of Joseph in which Jesus was buried.

walls built in the Middle Ages by Suleiman the Magnificent. If the traditional site is correct it would have had to have been outside the walls of New Testament Jerusalem (Heb. 13:12). Since we are not certain of the direction of this part of the wall of Jesus' day, the question is still an open one.

In 1883 General Charles Gordon, a devout Christian who had distinguished himself in British army service, noted the rocky hill about 250 yards northeast of the Damascus Gate and suggested that this might be the true site of Calvary. It is outside the walls of Jerusalem, hence free from the problems presented by the traditional site. The configuration of the rock gives the appearance of a skull, suggesting the reason for the name Golgotha, "place of a skull." Nearby is a Roman tomb, now known as the Garden Tomb. It is said that the suggestion that this might be the true Calvary was first made by a man named Otto Thenius in 1849. It was Gordon's name and reputation that popularized the idea, however, and the site is preserved today as a beautiful garden in which Protestant worship services are frequently held.

Scholars have not taken seriously the claims of Gordon's Calvary. The tomb itself probably dates from the third century, and the skull-shaped rock is the result of quarrying carried on until comparatively recent times. While traditions concerning the Church of the Holy Sepulchre may not be thoroughly reliable, they seem stronger than those which associate the death and resurrection of Jesus with the so-called Gordon's Calvary. In our present state of knowledge, no identification is wholly satisfactory. A visit to the Herodian family tombs should satisfy the Christian who would like to know what a tomb with a rolling stone really looked like. That is the kind of stone that posed a problem to the women on that first Easter morning, until they learned that a power stronger than their own had rolled the stone away.

The generation between A.D. 30 and A.D. 70 saw the beginnings of the Christian church and the end of that Temple worship which had characterized Jewish life since the return from Babylonian Exile. Following the resurrection and ascension of Jesus, the earliest believers continued to live in Jerusalem. They had no thought of dissociating themselves from other Jews, but rather thought of themselves as Israelites who had recognized in Jesus of Nazareth their promised Messiah. As Jesus had clashed with both the Roman authorities and the religious leadership of the Jews, the Christians could hardly have expected

HERODIAN FAMILY TOMB in Jerusalem. The tomb shows a rolling stone such as was placed at the entrance of the tomb of Jesus (Cf. Mark 16:4). Courtesy, Gerald Larue

to go unnoticed. Apostles still went to the Temple at the times for prayer, but their preaching proved distasteful and attempts were made to silence them. They were threatened and imprisoned. Stephen, a deacon in the young church, preached with such power and aroused such antagonism that he was stoned to death.

Persecution, however, did not stop the Christian movement. A fresh encouragement came to the church when an ardent Pharisee, Saul of Tarsus, was converted and became Paul, the "apostle to the Gentiles," the Christian movement's most ardent missionary. Hebrew Christians continued to live and worship in Jerusalem, but Paul and his like-minded friends envisioned Christianity as a worldwide movement, embracing Jew and Gentile alike. Christianity went from Jerusalem to Judea and Samaria, and then to the uttermost parts of the (Roman) world within the lifetime of Paul.

In the meantime difficulties were shaping up in Jerusalem. Resentment against the presence of Romans in the Holy City ran high and political insurrection was in the air. Pharisees and Sadducees represented the parties of moderation, but the Zealot extremists gained the upper hand. Rome had given them ample reason to rebel. The climax came in A.D. 66 when a band of Zealots seized the fortress of Massada on the western shore of the Dead Sea and equipped themselves from the huge arsenal of the fortress. Under their leader Menahem they next turned to Jerusalem.

During the feast of Succoth, when Jerusalem was jammed with pilgrims, the Zealots entered the city and seized the Fortress Antonia and Herod's Palace. Part of the city was burned, including the palaces of Agrippa and of the High Priest. Menahem was captured and killed, but new leaders continued the war. Cestius Gallus, the Legate of Syria, had the nearest Roman army but his response to the Jewish revolt was slow. He finally entered Jerusalem and reached the environs of the Temple, but he realized his vulnerable position in an enemy country and withdrew. In the autumn of A.D. 66 he was defeated in a battle with the Jews at the Descent of Beth-Horon and lost his siege train and all his war matériel.

Jerusalem faced no further external threats until Passover of A.D. 70. The insurrection had spread into Galilee where a man named Josephus tried to take a moderate position. Ultimately

INSCRIPTION OF THE TENTH ROMAN LEGION, discovered at Abu Ghosh, Old Testament Kirjath-Jearim, west of Jerusalem. The Tenth Legion entered and destroyed Jerusalem in A.D. 70. Courtesy, Gerald Larue

he made his peace with the Romans and became the historian of the Jewish War. The extremist leader in Galilee, John of Giscala, fled to Jerusalem where the extremists overthrew the government of the High Priests and fought among themselves for power.

When Titus, son and heir to the emperor Vespasian, arrived with an army of four Roman legions, the Zealots abandoned their jockeying for power and set about strengthening the city. Titus came from the north, but the Jews were unable to stop him. Since there was a shortage of wood, the Romans cut down every tree in the district. They brought in war machines and began to bombard the city. Early in May a breach was opened in the northern wall and Titus moved in to become master of the Bethezda quarter in the northeast. The Romans continued their advance, and ten days later they took the second wall. The Jews still held the Antonia, the Temple, and the western quarter of the city, so Titus decided to starve them out. The Jewish quarter suffered almost beyond human endurance, but the Jews refused to surrender. Titus finally decided to force submission. Late in June he took the Fortress Antonia and razed it to the ground. Early in July the Temple fell, bringing to an end the daily sacrifices which had been offered for centuries on its altars. Titus tried to spare the Temple, but his soldiers threw a lighted torch through the window and set the sanctuary on fire. Titus saved the menorah — the seven-branched candlestick — which he carried with him in his triumph at Rome. The Temple itself was a total loss when Titus' armies retired on August 6.

The last resistance in the western part of the city was overcome by the beginning of September. Herod's three towers, the Hippicus, the Phasael, and the Mariamne, were spared to serve as barracks for the Tenth Roman Legion. Otherwise the destruction was complete. In A.D. 71 Titus celebrated his triumph in Rome. The Romans struck a coin with the inscription "Conquered Judea," depicting a woman weeping by a palm tree.

7

THE ROMANS AND THE PERSIANS

After the carnage of A.D. 70, Titus returned to Rome where he enjoyed a great triumph. His arch in Rome still shows Titus bringing booty from Jerusalem. The seven-branched golden candlestick is clearly visible. Although Titus destroyed the Temple he rescued its treasures for his triumph. He brought with him the sacred scrolls of the law. More important, seven hundred Jewish prisoners walked behind the Zealot leader Simon Bar-Giora in the victory parade. The celebration reached its climax in the execution of Simon.

The destruction of the Temple brought an end to the rituals which were associated with it. No longer did priests approach altars with sacrificial victims. The Babylonian exile had proved that the Jew could survive without a Temple, and the destruction of Jerusalem made it necessary for him to do so. A Jewish leader of these times was Johanan ben Zakkai, whose father had been a pupil of the great Rabbi Hillel. Legend states that Johanan asked Titus for permission to settle, with his followers, in Jamnia — about 30 miles west of Jerusalem. Johanan had not been a part of the Zealot movement which had defied Rome, and Titus did not interfere with the Jamnia settlement. The Jews at Jamnia constituted a Sanhedrin, or council of elders, and devoted their time to the study of the Law and its application to their contemporary problems. The rabbis at Jamnia gave their attention to the canon of Scripture. The result of their discussions was the acceptance without further question of the books which comprise the Christian Old Testament, the Jewish "Law, Prophets, and Writings." Not only was the Old Testament then

49

TRIUMPHAL ARCH OF TITUS in Rome, commemorating the Roman victory over Israel in A.D. 70. Courtesy, Italian State Tourist Office

THE EMPEROR HADRIAN.
Courtesy, National Museum,
Naples

codified, but the Jamnia rabbis began that body of commentary and explanation which came to be known as the Talmud.

Jerusalem remained in ruins, but pious Jews still looked to it as the Holy City. Some would make their way to the ruins of the Temple to worship, much as their descendants prayed for centuries at the Wailing Wall. When Hadrian became emperor (A.D. 117) the Jews looked upon him as a second Cyrus who might permit them to rebuild the city of their fathers. Hadrian was a lover of antiquity, and he made it a policy to restore ruined cities. In A.D. 130 he visited the ruins of Jerusalem, and soon afterward he began the work of restoration. It was not as Jerusalem, the city of the Jews, that he intended to rebuild the city, however, but as Aelia Capitolina, the city of Hadrian (whose full name was Aelius Publius Hadrianus) and the Capitoline Triad — the principal deities of Rome. A temple of Jupiter was to be built on the site of the ruined Jewish Temple.

Loyal Jews were horrified at Hadrian's plans, which seemed a conscious profanation of the Holy City. At about the same time Hadrian issued an edict against mutilation, aimed particularly at those non-Jewish sects which practiced self-disfigurement. The Jews, however, interpreted this as an attack upon their rite of circumcision. Desecration of their city and proscription of their laws aroused the latent anti-Roman feeling among the Jews. A Zealot leader known as Simon Bar-Kokhba ("son of the star" — a messianic title) became Israel's new champion. The revered scholar Rabbi Akiba proclaimed him Israel's Messiah, and thousands believed him to be the anointed of the Lord who would drive out the Romans and vindicate the faith of Israel.

During the early days of the revolt (A.D. 132-135) the Jews had the initiative. Bar-Kokhba's forces overran the Judean Plain and cut off the Roman garrison in Jerusalem from its commander, the governor of Judea, in Caesarea. The Roman Legion and Roman civilians were driven from Jerusalem and it was again a Jewish city with some form of Temple worship carried on at the site of the old Temple. Roman armies waited in their fortresses until fresh recruits arrived. Hadrian summoned his chief general Sextus Julius Severus to conduct his campaign in Palestine. By A.D. 134 the Roman armies were closing in on the Jews. Bar-Kokhba had to evacuate Jerusalem. Resistance continued at Beit-Ter (Bettir), but within a year Rome was completely victorious.

The revolt had failed. The Romans determined to prevent the Jews from having another opportunity to assert their independence. Jewish slaves were sold in marketplaces throughout the East. Aelia Capitolina was to be a Roman city and, under penalty of death, no Jew was to approach its environs. The name Judea was ordered abandoned and Hadrian gave the name Syria Palestina — Syria of the Philistines — to southern Syria.

Aelia Capitolina was a beautiful city with white columns and colonnades. Its wall was built on roughly the lines of the old Jewish city, but the new city's distinctive features were its forum, theater, and baths. The Temple area, named *Qadra* ("The Square"), had a Temple to the Capitoline Triad — Jupiter Capitolinus, Juno, and Venus-Aphrodite. A statue of Hadrian stood at its front entrance.

During the second and third centuries, Aelia was a typically Roman city. Except for the banished Jews (including Jewish Christians) its religious life was cosmopolitan. Oriental gods, including Serapis, were worshiped. By the third century Gentile Christian pilgrims began to appear in Palestine to visit "the city of Christ." In A.D. 212 Bishop Alexander Flavian journeyed from Cappadocia to the Holy Land. The middle of the third century found Origen active in the Christian churches of Palestine. Persecutions under Diocletian and Maximinus (303-311) made life difficult for the Christians, but a new day began in 326 when Helena, the Christian mother of the Emperor Constantine, journeyed to Jerusalem and other sacred sites. Legend states that Helena discovered the "true cross" in what became the crypt of the Church of the Holy Sepulchre. Fifth-century writers state that she discovered three crosses, and that the true one was authenticated by a miracle. According to one version a sick person was healed upon touching the cross on which Jesus was crucified. Another states that a dead man was resurrected when touched by the cross. Tradition says that Macarius, bishop of Aelia (d. *ca.* 334), under orders from Constantine, excavated at the site of the Roman Temple of Aphrodite and discovered the tomb of Christ. The first Church of the Holy Sepulchre was built over the site. Helena was also responsible for the building of the Church of the Nativity on the traditional site of the birth of Jesus, and the Eleona, or Church of the Olive Trees, on the Mount of Olives. A fourth-century Christian known simply as the Pilgrim of Bordeaux tells us that he saw the basilicas in the course of their erection. The church historian Eusebius, bishop of Caesarea, knew the city of Aelia and asserted that the church there was composed entirely of Gentiles because of the expulsion of the Jews. Late in the fourth century a Spanish pilgrim named Etheria visited various Eastern countries including the Holy Land. She describes the Holy Week and Easter observances in Jerusalem, including the procession with palms to the Mount of Olives, and the Veneration of the Cross.

As pilgrimages became popular, Aelia Capitolina — now being called by its old name, Jerusalem, again — became an important Christian center. Pilgrims came to see the so-called holy places and, if possible, to bring to their native churches some sacred relic. Persuasive guides were ever ready to locate the sites of events recorded in both the Old and New Testaments. Pilgrims were shown the sycamore tree into which Zacchaeus climbed or the very pillar where Jesus had been scourged — with the brown stains of his blood still there! When we remember the destruction of the city in A.D. 70 and again in 135 we see how little credence should be given to such speculations. Pilgrims wanted to see the sites, and guides were obliging.

Most shameful was the traffic in relics. Since Helena's discovery of the "true cross," pilgrims wanted to take home some of its sacred wood. To satisfy the demand, the custodians of the shrines manufactured the story that the cross had the supernatural power to multiply itself. Enough fragments were taken to Europe to have rebuilt Solomon's Temple. Cemeteries were looted to find the bones of the saints, and pieces of sacred skeletons found their way to the churches of Europe. A pilgrim could buy a "genuine" string from King David's harp or a tent "sewn" by the apostle Paul. A gullible Christian purchased the adze used by Noah in building the ark. Gallons of Jordan River water were jugged and prepared for shipment — perhaps the most authentic of all the souvenirs which pilgrims took to Europe.

During the fourth century, Christianity moved from the status of an illicit religion to an acceptable religion (Constantine) to the official religion of the Empire (Theodosius, A.D. 379). As western Rome fell before the Goths, aristocrats and princes made their way to Jerusalem. New churches began to arise as the holy places were "identified." Above the Eleona, built by Helena, was the Imbomon marking the site of the Ascension. Holy Zion marked the supposed site of the Last Supper. A church in the Garden of Gethsemane marked the site (and the actual stone) where Jesus prayed before his betrayal. The Dormition stood where pilgrims believed the Virgin Mary "fell asleep."

THE GARDEN OF GETHSEMANE, west of Jerusalem on the slopes of
the Mount of Olives.

THE CHURCH OF ALL NATIONS in the Garden of Gethsemane, on
the slopes of the Mount of Olives.

Paganism was to have one more opportunity before its classical form would be buried forever. Julian, called "the Apostate," was proclaimed Emperor in A.D. 360. He was too wise and humane to persecute the Christian church openly, but he did remove all preferments and he placed Christians on the same level, legally, with pagans. Julian saw in Judaism a third force and he determined to restore to the Jews their Holy City and to rebuild the Temple. Thousands of Jews returned to their homeland and the wealth of Babylon and Egypt was pledged to make the project successful.

The project came to an end in a way that the Christians deemed miraculous. Julian's workers attempted to enter an underground passage while carrying a torch. Explosive sewer gas had gathered in the cavern and the fire of the torch ignited it, causing an explosion. The laborers fled and would not return. Christians were convinced that their Lord had shown his displeasure at the project, and Julian's death in 363 confirmed them in their faith. For three centuries Jerusalem was to be a center of Christendom. Pilgrimages were encouraged and Jews were allowed in Jerusalem only on the ninth of Ab — the anniversary of the destruction of their Temple.

In 438 the Empress Eudocia, wife of Theodosius II, made a pilgrimage to Jerusalem. Eudocia, the daughter of an Athenian professor of rhetoric, was a woman of culture and wealth. During the few months she was in Jerusalem, Eudocia was known for the alms she distributed. She brought relics with her when she returned home, and she continued her interest in the construction of new churches in Jerusalem: Saint Sophia of the Praetorium, Saint Peter of the Palace of Caiaphas ("The Church of the Renunciation"), Saint John the Baptist, and the church of Siloam, near the pool into which Hezckiah's tunnel leads.

After being estranged from her husband, Eudocia returned to Jerusalem (ca. 442) and spent the last twenty years of her life there. She is remembered for the churches, monasteries, and hospices she endowed. Her generosity was not limited to church affairs, however. Since Hadrian's time, Jerusalem had not been protected by walls. Lack of adequate defense would pose a serious problem in a time of invasion, so Theodosius II began to rebuild the walls in 413. Eudocia completed the work, and she is usually credited with the Golden Gate, now walled up, to the east of the Temple area. The Golden Gate was built on the site identified as the place where Peter and Paul healed a lame man who was going into the Temple. Eudocia retained her rank as Empress and her royal revenues after her separation from Theodosius II. Under her wise rule the Jews were permitted to return to Jerusalem and settle there. Some had come earlier, but Eudocia's decree made their settlement legal.

Eudocia found herself enmeshed in the religious quarrels which were to weaken the church and prepare the way for its subjection to Islam in the Holy Land. Following the Council of Chalcedon (451), the churches of Egypt and Syria found themselves at odds with the official position of Byzantium. The Council of Chalcedon affirmed that Jesus was One Person in Two Natures, united unconfusedly, unchangeably, indivisibly, inseparably. The so-called Monophysites of the East taught that there was but a single — and that a Divine — Nature in the Person of the Incarnate Christ. There were, of course, political as well as theological overtones to the schisms throughout the East. The power of Byzantium was resented, and one way to attack it was through the church. The Egyptian Copts, with the related Ethiopian Church; the Syrian Jacobites (named for their leader Jacob Baradaeus); and (unofficially) the Armenian Church are Monophysite in theology. All repudiate the Council of Chalcedon, while accepting the decisions of the church fathers prior to Chalcedon. The differences persist to this day and are most noticeable in the rivalries of five church bodies for space and "rights" in the Church of the Holy Sepulchre.

Although shaken by the Monophysite controversy, Byzantium still dreamed of a unified empire with Constantinople, its capital, serving as a new Rome. Justinian (527-565) deemed himself the elect of God, predestined to govern the world. Early in his reign Justinian had to turn his attention toward Palestine because of a revolt of the Samaritans who had been suffering under a crushing burden of taxation. Relief came, and Justinian undertook to rebuild churches that had been destroyed and to erect a hospital for sick pilgrims in Jerusalem.

With the patronage of Justinian, the patriarch Peter directed the building of a great church known as Saint Mary the New. Work continued from 531 to 543 on the structure, built on the western hill of Jerusalem. The church was approached by colonnades and framed by porticoes on either side. Nothing, however, remains today. Even the exact location is uncertain.

The Jerusalem of Justinian's time is represented on a mosaic map discovered at Madaba in Jordan (ancient Moab) in 1884. Above the representation of the city in red letters we read, "The Holy City Jerusalem." The city is oval shaped, surrounded by walls with six gates. Streets are colonnaded. The principal building in the city is the Anastasis, known today as the Church of the Holy Sepulchre. Four steps lead up to the façade of the basilica, which has three doors. A golden dome stands over the rotunda of the church, marking the site of the tomb of Jesus. In all, thirty-six buildings are represented in the city, including churches, monasteries, palaces, and public buildings.

Justinian's Jerusalem was a wealthy city. The treasures of Christendom had poured into it. Christian pilgrims came to worship and admire, but others looked with lusting eyes upon the wealth of the city. Christian Jerusalem was at its zenith in Justinian's time. Soon the Persian, and then the Arab, would tread her streets.

In A.D. 227 the Sassanian King Ardaschir dethroned the last Parthian king and attempted a revival of the Persian Empire of Darius and Xerxes. Zoroastrianism was the official religion of Persia. Since Roman rulers attempted to maintain the Euphrates River as their eastern boundary, sooner or later the interests of Persia and Byzantium were bound to clash. After Constantine, the Roman (Byzantine) Empire was identified with Christianity, just as Persia was identified with Zoroastrianism. The conflicts between Persians and Byzantines thus took on religious overtones.

The Euphrates was a tenuous border for Roman power; it could not be defended easily, and the population throughout Syria was basically Oriental. In 606, Chosroes II Parviz ("The Victorious") of Persia invaded Mesopotamia, and the following year he ravaged Syria and Palestine. Although Heraclius, son of the Byzantine governor of Africa, was able to save the day for Byzantium when he seized power in 610, Chosroes was still powerful enough to strike again. In 612 the Persians were in Cappadocia and Armenia. Persians received the support of Jews who had been persecuted by the Byzantine Empire as Chosroes entered Damascus, Aleppo, and Antioch in 613. The Persians asked the patriarch Zachariah in Jerusalem to surrender and he wanted to do so until one faction in the city demanded a policy of resistance. A garrison came from Jericho to help raise the siege, but it soon retired. The Persians lighted fires close to the walls of the city and brought up their battering rams. On May 20, 614, the walls were breached and Jerusalem was taken by storm. Conservative accounts state that 33,877 people were slain. All the monasteries were burned and the churches were left in ruins. Three hundred years of construction were obliterated. The Church of the Holy Sepulchre, known to the Greeks as the Anastasis, dating from the time of Constantine, and the beautiful Saint Mary the New, from the time of Justinian, were destroyed beyond recognition. Many of the survivors were taken as prisoners to Persia. Among them was the patriarch Zachariah with the "true cross" which he had rescued.

The Persians controlled Palestine until 629, but during those years the Christians were able to rebuild some of their shrines. The Anastasis was provided with a new dome and the basilica itself was restored on a scale more modest than that of the earlier building. Other churches, including the Eleona and Saint Sophia, were not rebuilt.

In the meantime Heraclius determined to push the battle into the enemy's home country. He bypassed the Persian army in Asia Minor and in 627 encamped before the Persian capital of Ctesiphon. Chosroes died in 628, but it was not until 629 that Heraclius concluded a peace treaty with Siroes, the new Persian king. At last his provinces were restored, prisoners were freed, and the "true cross" was back in Jerusalem. Heraclius personally restored the relic, carrying it on foot from the Golden Gate to the Anastasis.

While Persia and Byzantium, Zoroastrian and Christian were exhausting themselves in battle, a new political and religious force was arising in the deserts of Arabia. The Christian might celebrate the liberation of Jerusalem from the Persian, but he was soon to face a fresh humiliation at the hand of the Muslim. The dream of a united Christendom controlling the extent of the old Roman Empire was never to become a reality.

8

THE MUSLIM AND THE CRUSADER

While Byzantine was fighting Persian, and orthodox Christian was struggling with Monophysite Christian, a new political and religious movement was coming into being in the wastes of Arabia. The Arabians were a Semitic people that had been bypassed by the great cultural movements that had challenged Syria and Palestine since the time of Alexander. Neither Greek nor Roman had penetrated the Arabian wastes. Border regions had been Christianized and had come under Byzantine influence, but for the most part Arabia was a heterogeneous group of miniature kingdoms and tribes with no common loyalty.

All this was changed by a man who was born about 570 in the trading center of Mecca. Mecca was a stronghold of the Quraish clan, and it was noted particularly for its shrine, the Kaaba. In Muhammad's time the Kaaba was a repository for 360 stone idols, a witness to the idolatry of the Quraish. Muhammad was raised by his uncle, Abu Talib, who was a trader. With his uncle, young Muhammad is thought to have made several trips into Syria where he met both Jews and Christians. While such contacts seem to have been superficial, Muhammad was evidently influenced by the Biblical traditions to which he was introduced. Christians and Jews, as People of the Book, were given a certain respect in Islam, although Muhammad insisted that both religions had falsified their Scriptures to expurgate references to himself.

After his marriage to the wealthy Khadija, Muhammad continued to make trips to the north of Arabia, and his knowledge of Christianity and Judaism continued to grow. At about the age of forty he felt himself called to the prophetic office. Three years passed before he received the first of a series of revelations

which were later gathered together and published as the Koran.
  Muhammad taught that there is but one God, Allah, and that
Muhammad was the last and chief of the prophets. Abraham,
Moses, Jesus, and others are regarded as earlier prophets, and
they are honored in Islam. Muhammad, however, found that his
message was not welcome among his kinsmen of the Quraish
tribe and he had to leave his native Mecca. In the year 622 he
fled to Yathrib, later known as Medina (i.e., "the city" of the
prophet), an event which is known as the Hejira. Medina
responded to Muhammad's message, and after seven years he
led an army of ten thousand back to Mecca to conquer the city
and destroy its idols.
  By the time of Muhammad's death (632) the faith of Islam
("submission" to God's will) had welded together the Arab
tribes. They were united in religion and they became a cohesive
political force to challenge the tired empires of the Mediterranean
basin. Neither Persia nor Byzantium could check their power.
  The year 634 found Omar, Muhammad's second successor,
attacking the territory of the Byzantine Emperor Heraclius. In
August of 635, Damascus fell to Omar and Heraclius raised an
army to destroy the forces which seemed but a short time before
to be little more than a nuisance. The decisive battle was fought
at the Yarmuk River in August, 636. Omar was able to bribe
two legions of Christian Arabs to leave the Byzantine army and
join his own. The Christians, Monophysite in faith, and hence
unsympathetic with the emperor's religious policy, swung the
tide of battle. Omar defeated the Byzantine army and he was
able to move into Syria and Palestine without further trouble.
  The Christian patriarch in Jerusalem, Sophronius, attempted to
defend the city, but he soon realized that it would prove futile
to do so. Sacred relics were dispatched to Byzantium for safe
keeping. The "true cross," however — the most sacred of all —
was buried in Jerusalem for safe keeping.
  Jerusalem, the city sacred to both Jew and Christian, was to
become Islam's third sacred city, along with Mecca and Medina.
A passage in the Koran was interpreted to mean that the angel
Gabriel had taken the prophet on a winged horse from Jerusalem to heaven itself. This, added to the veneration due the
city because of associations with earlier prophets honored in
Islam, made Omar and his generals anxious to avoid battle if at
all possible.
  The Arab commander addressed a letter to Sophronius from
his camp in the Jordan Valley. The Christians were urged to

surrender and they were offered the choice of embracing Islam or paying heavy tribute. Sophronius rejected the surrender bid, but when the Arab armies actually surrounded Jerusalem he had second thoughts. The Christian leader declared that he would capitulate only to the Caliph Omar personally. Omar made the journey north from Medina, and the Caliph and the Patriarch met on the Mount of Olives. The terms of surrender were as generous as any in the long history of Jerusalem. Christians who did not embrace Islam were to be guaranteed safety and the right to their property as long as they paid their taxes and did not interfere with the Muslim faith. The existing churches could continue their services, but they had to be open at all times for inspection. No new churches or other religious edifices were to be built. Bells were not to be sounded and the sign of the cross was not to be displayed publicly. Christians were not to adopt the dress, customs, or language of the conquerors, nor to take Arabic names.

When the terms were agreed upon, Sophronius led Omar into the city. The patriarch is reported to have said, "This is the abomination of desolation," in the presence of Omar, but the Muslims did not comprehend its meaning and assumed that Omar's victory had been prophesied in the Christian Scriptures.

THE OLD CITY OF JERUSALEM, with the Dome of the Rock in the foreground.

Sophronius took Omar first to the Anastasis — the Church of the Holy Sepulchre. Legend states that they arrived at the hour of prayer, but Omar refused to pray, stating that if he were to do so the Christians would lose their shrine. Faithful Muslims would say, "Omar prayed here," and make it a holy place. The Caliph was anxious to see the Temple area because of its association with Abraham who prepared to offer his son Isaac there. Christians had sought to insult the Jews by making the ruins of the Temple area a municipal garbage dump. Legend suggests that a renegade Jew pointed out the sacred rock to the Caliph. Omar ordered his attendants to clear away the refuse and he determined to build a mosque on the site. The building known as the Mosque of Omar or, more correctly, the Dome of the Rock, was not built at this time. It was erected by Abd al-Malik in the year 691. Omar's tastes were simpler and he is said to have ordered a simple wooden mosque over the rock which was discovered under the refuse of Jerusalem. Except for the period of the Crusades, Jerusalem has been a Muslim city since the time of Omar, although it remains sacred to the Christian and the Jew as well.

The burden of Arab rule was light during the early years. Byzantine officials continued to rule under Arab supervision. Sophronius died in 639 and the patriarchate remained vacant until 706. With the passing of the years, Muslim control gradually increased.

The Muslim appropriation of the old Temple area removed any hopes the Jews may have had for a new Jewish temple. Jews were allowed to return to Jerusalem, however, and soon after the Arab conquest the *Gaonim*, who constituted the highest Jewish religious authority in Palestine, moved from Tiberias to Jerusalem where they remained until the eleventh century. Jews lived in their own quarter of the city where they had their own synagogues. They went to the Wailing Wall to lament the passing of former glories and to pray for their restoration.

Christians maintained their churches and holy places in Jerusalem and throughout the Muslim world. Syrian and Greek Christians were found useful as civil servants in the courts of some of the califs. The Muslim conquerors were wise enough to avail themselves of the training and administrative experience of the subject peoples. Christians in the employ of the califs looked to the Byzantine emperor as the Defender of the Faith.

Since the Muslims acknowledged Jerusalem as their third holy city, they took the old Temple area and built there a group of sacred buildings. Most important was the Dome of the Rock, commemorating the site where Abraham prepared to offer Isaac and where, in Muslim tradition, Muhammad ascended to heaven on his horse Baraq. Biblical scholars suggest that the rock also marked the site of the Holy of Holies of the Jewish Temple.

The fifth Ummayad caliph, Abd al-Malik, had both political and religious reasons for building the Dome of the Rock. A rival had deprived him of the holy cities of Arabia, so he determined to divert religious interest in Mecca to Jerusalem. By building a beautiful structure, he also desired to give the Muslims a monument of their own that would cause them to take pride in their own faith and resist the temptation to apostatize in favor of Christianity.

The cupola was begun in 687 and, although additional ornamentation and repairs have been made several times since then, the present structure is essentially that of Abd al-Malik. The architecture is Byzantine in form, with a style comparable to that of the Anastasis and the Ascension rotundas. The artists and artisans employed in the construction of the Dome of the Rock were probably Syrians who had been influenced by Greek style in architecture. The dome is 65 feet wide. It rests on four pillars and eight circular columns. The building is octagonal in shape with four gates. There is an inner octagon with eight pillars and sixteen columns.

Surrounded by a railing is the sacred rock itself, believed during the Middle Ages to mark the center of a round, flat earth. Adjacent to the rock is a subterranean cave, actually hewn out of the rock, where Muslims believe the souls of the dead assemble for prayer.

In 1016 the dome was shattered by an earthquake and replaced with a new one. Blue Persian tiles and stained glass windows date from the sixteenth century. Within the past few years the dome has been gilded so that it now gleams brightly in the sun.

The nearby Al-Aqsa Mosque may be on the site of Justinian's church, known as Saint Mary the New. It was built at the southern end of the Haram, or sacred enclosure, by the Ummayid Caliph Al-Walid. Ruins of the former church were doubtless used in its construction. The result was a large structure with 280 columns, a cupola, and beautiful mosaics.

Jerusalem got along quite well as long as power remained in the Ummayid dynasty of califs, who ruled from Damascus. Things were not as pleasant, however, after 763 when the

Abbasid dynasty moved the Arab capital to Baghdad. With the center of power moved eastward, Jerusalem was to face new threats and challenges.

The Eastern, or Byzantine, remnant of the Roman Empire was forced to accept the fact of Muslim dominance in western Asia, but she still had dreams of consolidating the European territories once ruled from Rome. Since Byzantium was looked upon as a threat to the emerging kingdoms in France, Germany, and Italy, the rival Islamic power was considered a potential ally. In the year 800 Charlemagne reestablished (in name, at least) the Western Roman Empire and opposed Byzantine claims in Italy. Charlemagne entered into diplomatic relations with the calif Haroun al-Rashid, famed for his part in the stories of the Arabian Nights. Haroun al-Rashid sent relics to Charlemagne and, according to legend, presented him with the keys to the Church of the Holy Sepulchre, acknowledging him rather than Nicephorus of Byzantium to be the defender of Jerusalem's holy places. It was in this way that the Latin, or Roman Catholic, Church gained recognition in the Holy Land. In exchange for the relics he received, Charlemagne gave gifts to Jerusalem and established Latin foundations there. To this day the Roman Catholics are termed Latins throughout the Bible lands.

Early pilgrims were largely from eastern Europe — the area of the Byzantine empire and the Eastern Orthodox churches. With the establishment of cordial relations between the Islamic rulers and the West, pilgrims from France, Britain, Germany, and Italy became more numerous. Members of the monastic order of Cluny, in Burgundy, encouraged pilgrimages as means of spiritual growth. Nobles such as the Count of Anjou, the Count of Verdun, the Archbishop of Mainz, and the Duke of Normandy led pilgrimages to Jerusalem for the spiritual edification of the faithful. Sometimes pilgrimages were prescribed as a means of penance for the careless.

While Cluny was encouraging pilgrimages in the West, the infamous Fatimid Calif Hakim came into control of the Islamic state. Although his mother had been a Christian, Hakim began his reign by passing legislation designed to oppress and humiliate the Christians of Syria and Palestine. He confiscated church property and, in the year 1009, ordered the destruction of the Church of the Holy Sepulchre. Thirty thousand Christian buildings are said to have been destroyed in Asia Minor and a mass slaughter of Christians was threatened. Thousands of Christians embraced Islam to save their lives.

In the year 1016 Hakim completely reversed himself. He removed the ordinances against Christians and permitted them to observe their faith without hindrance. At the same time, Hakim announced to his people that he was Allah — the god they had been worshiping. His own name was to be substituted for that of Allah in the sacred writings of Islam, and in all prayers and devotions. His last act was an edict forbidding Muslims to make the pilgrimage to Mecca. Thereupon the Muslims themselves arose against him, forced him to flee and, according to legend, he found refuge in the forests of Lebanon. Some say that his sister, with a band of assassins, found him and killed him. The sect known as the Druses honors his memory and expects him to return to earth. Otherwise, he left no mark upon Islam.

Stories of Hakim's oppression of Christians and desecration of the Holy Places reached Europe, however. When Pope Sergius IV heard of the destruction of the Church of the Holy Sepulchre, he issued a bull urging Christian retaliation for the infamous crime. Sergius had no thought of launching a crusade, but he did make Western Christendom conscious of the problems of the East. It was not until the end of the century before Pope Urban II called upon the kings and nobles of Europe to join a war against the Infidels to rescue the Holy Places. Urban was astute enough to realize that such a venture would compel the warring princes to unite in a common cause. Instead of plundering one another's land, they could seize Asia Minor, Syria, and Palestine from the "Infidel." Religious fervor certainly motivated some of the crusaders, but many came for baser reasons.

On November 27, 1095, Urban built up his case against Islam in a synodical meeting at Clermont in France. Christians were asked to lay down their work and begin the trek toward Jerusalem. All who marched under the Crusader's banner with its cross of red would receive full absolution of all their sins! The crowd cried out, *"Deus vult! Deus vult!"* ("God wills it! God wills it!")

By the ninth century, the Abbasid dynasty had weakened as the result of the growing power of the Seljuk Turks. The Seljuks had been hired by the Arabs as mercenary soldiers, but they ultimately became rulers of the empire. They took Jerusalem in 1071 and immediately began to harass the Christian pilgrims, exacting heavy tolls from them.

The Seljuk Turks posed both a religious and a political threat to Byzantium. They occupied most of Asia Minor and threatened

THE DOME OF THE ASCENSION on the Mount of Olives. The structure was built by the Crusaders on the site of the ancient Imbomon. It is a Moslem mosque today.

THE DOME OF THE ROCK, sometimes called the Mosque of Omar, on the sight of the ancient Temple.

THE BELLS OF THE CHURCH OF THE HOLY SEPULCHRE form the frame for a view over the rooftops of Jerusalem to the Mount of Olives. The Dome of the Rock is in the right foreground. Courtesy, Jordan Tourist Department

Constantinople and eastern Europe. A Byzantine army was sent to fight the Turks at Jerusalem, but it ended in disaster for the Christians. Appeals were made to Popes Gregory VII and Urban II. The appeal of the Byzantine Emperor, Alexius I Comnenus, to Urban was one reason Urban proposed his crusade at Clermont.

Preachers, including the famous Peter the Hermit, went throughout Europe urging people to help in the recovery of the Holy Land. A motley crowd — scarcely an army — made its way to Constantinople, living off the land and stealing when necessary. To the cultured Byzantines, the Franks (as all Crusaders were called) appeared thoroughly uncouth. Princess Anna Comnena wrote:

> Now the Frankish counts are naturally shameless and violent, naturally greedy of money, too, and immoderate in everything they wish, and possess a flow of language greater than any other human race; and they did not make their visits to the emperor in any order, but each count as he came brought in as many men as he liked with him; and one came after another, and another in turn after him. And when they came in, they did not regulate their conversation by a waterglass, as the rule was for orators formerly, but for as long as each wished to talk to the emperor, be he even a mere nobody, for so long he was allowed to talk.[1]

In marching through Europe the Crusaders had wreaked havoc. Jews were slaughtered in their Rhineland communities on the pretext that the Crusaders were avenging the death of Christ. Rape, thievery, and arson were practiced with the thought that the indulgences granted to Crusaders guaranteed pardon for such sins. Many of the Crusaders were highminded Christians, to be sure, but the half-barbarian opportunists gave the whole movement a horrible reputation in Europe as well as in the Holy Land.

After passing through Asia Minor with considerable difficulty, the Crusaders reached Antioch in the fall of 1097. Antioch, one of the great cities of the world, felt safe behind the walls erected by Justinian. The Crusaders — estimated at 300,000 men — laid siege to the city, but months went by and Antioch stood firm. The Crusaders themselves suffered for lack of food, but they continued the siege until success was attained. One of the captains of the city, a Christian, let down a ladder during the night

---

1 Quoted in J. B. Ross and M. M. McLaughlin, ed., *The Portable Medieval Reader*, p. 445. (New York: 1949).

and the Crusader Bohemond of Otranto and a hundred of his
men climbed into Antioch. The city was taken and the Turkish
garrison sent to repulse the Crusaders was defeated. The Crusaders were encouraged by the discovery of a lance which was
reputed to have been the one that wounded Christ. This ap-
parent evidence of God's blessing spurred them on to fresh
enthusiasm as they planned to attack Jerusalem.

Antioch fell in June, 1098, and the Crusaders decided to wait
until fall before completing their journey. They left Antioch in
November and fought their way southward, not arriving outside
Jerusalem until June, 1099. Although it was again summer, the
worst time of the year for fighting in the Bible Lands, they
immediately besieged the city. After six frustrating weeks of
siege, Peter the Hermit brought a message supposedly sent by
one of the Crusaders who had died the year before at Antioch.
The nobles must abandon their wrangling and the people must
march around Jerusalem each day for nine days. Then the city
would fall.

While some of the Crusaders were setting up siege machinery
against the walls of Jerusalem, a host of pilgrims marched around
the walls of the city singing hymns and shouting their prayers.
The defenders of the city taunted the Christians, oblivious to the
fact that the Crusaders were preparing to attack. On July 15
the siege engines were completed and the battle began. Scaling
ladders were raised and advance guards fought their way into
the city to open the gates for their comrades.

An eyewitness has given us an account of the events that
follow:

> Entering the city, our pilgrims pursued and killed Saracens up to
> the Temple of Solomon,[2] in which they had assembled and where
> they gave battle to us furiously for the whole day so that their
> blood flowed throughout the whole temple. Finally, having over-
> come the pagans, our knights seized a great number of men and
> women, and they killed whom they wished and whom they wished
> they let live. . . . Soon the Crusaders ran throughout the city,
> seizing gold, silver, horses, mules, and houses full of all kinds of
> goods. Then rejoicing and weeping our men went to worship
> at the sepulchre of our Savior Jesus and thus fulfill our pledge to
> Him. . . .
> Then our knights decided in council that each one should give
> alms with prayers so that God should elect whom He wished to
> reign over the others and rule the city. They also ordered that

---

2 The Crusaders called the Dome of the Rock "The Temple of Solomon."

all of the Saracen dead should be thrown out of the city because
of the extreme stench, for the city was almost full of their cadavers.
The live Saracens dragged the dead out before the gates and
made piles of them, like houses. No one has ever heard of or
seen such a slaughter of pagan peoples since pyres were made of
them like boundary marks, and no one except God knows their
number.[3]

Islam has not forgotten that massacre. Neither Omar in 638
nor Saladin in 1187 were guilty of such carnage. Jew and
Muslim alike met their death on that fateful day, for the Jews
were burned to death in their synagogue. Godfrey of Bouillon
was given the title "Defender of the Holy Sepulchre." He was,
in fact, governor of Jerusalem. On his death in 1100 he was
succeeded by his brother Baldwin, who established the Latin
Kingdom of Jerusalem.

Following the massacre of 1099 Jerusalem became a Christian
city. Both European and Syrian Christians were encouraged to
settle in the city, although the Crusaders attempted to impose
their feudal system upon their holdings in Palestine. Muslims
were deprived of their mosques and reduced to the status of
servants or slaves of the Christians. As time went on the Eastern
Christians and the Muslims developed better relations, but the
Franks made no effort to find an accommodation with the people
they had conquered. As a result, they continued to be an alien
people, given sullen obedience when necessary but generally
hated.

If the Crusaders were a failure in the area of political acumen
they were a success in the field of architecture. On July 15, 1149
— the fiftieth anniversary of the conquest — they dedicated the
reconstructed Church of the Holy Sepulchre. The rebuilt church
was designed to incorporate the traditional Calvary as well as the
tomb of Jesus. The earlier Anastasis was preserved and the
small church containing the traditional sepulchre was rebuilt.
Then a two-storied chapel was built to contain the Calvary sum-
mit. The whole group was richly adorned with mosaics. Godfrey of Bouillon and his first three successors were buried in
this enduring monument to their reigns.

Godfrey lived in the Mosque el-Aqsa until more suitable quar-
ters could be provided on the site of Herod's Citadel. The Dome
of the Rock was headquarters for the Templar Order who took
the title "Guardians of the Temple" in the belief that the

3 *Historie anonyme de la premiere croisade*, L. Brehier, ed. (Paris: Champion, 1924). Quoted in *Portable Medieval Reader*, p. 443.

structure then standing was actually Solomon's Temple. Another order, the Knights Hospitaler of St. John of Jerusalem built their headquarters near the Church of the Holy Sepulchre. These two orders, popularly known as Templars and Hospitalers, had been created to guard pilgrims in their journeys from Europe to the Holy Land against Muslim assault. The knights took vows of obedience, poverty, and chastity, and they were highly re-

THE HOLY SEPULCHRE, traditional site of the burial place of Jesus in the Church of the Holy Sepulchre.

THE CHURCH OF SAINT ANNE, dating to Crusader times. To the right are excavations of the Pool of Bethesda.

garded in the early days of their existence. In time they became wealthy and lost much of the respect given them in early years. The orders were active in the program of church building which was carried on during the first decades of the Latin Kingdom.

Between 1099 and 1187, when the Crusaders were forced out of Jerusalem, the city could boast of thirty-seven churches, many of them built or rebuilt during this time. One of the finest still standing is the Church of Saint Anne, just inside St. Stephen's Gate and near the ancient Pool of Bethesda. Saint Anne's is considered the finest example of Crusader architecture. It embodies a Romanesque style with Eastern elements in a most happy combination.

Crusader Jerusalem was enclosed within walls. It had four gates through which pilgrims and the local population made their way to trade in the markets or to worship in the churches. Small industries developed and Jews, who were gradually readmitted to the city, were engaged largely in the dyeing trade. The "Syrians" — the name given to Christians of oriental descent — operated the money changers' bazaar to meet the needs of pilgrims. In spite of centuries of change in the Old City of Jerusalem, many aspects of the city today would have seemed familiar to the Crusaders. The money changer is still there to service the needs of Americans, Europeans, and others who find continuing fascination in the city of Jerusalem.

Many of the Crusaders were disappointed with the terrain around the Holy City. This was not the fertile farm land to which they were accustomed and many were content to visit the Holy Places and then return to Europe. This, of course, was a source of weakness to the Latin Kingdom which was always alien to the Muslim world which surrounded it. The cities of Acre, Jaffa, and Caesarea were its lifeline, for the Crusaders were not able to support themselves off the land, or to maintain a resident army large enough to provide safety. The trading companies of Pisa, Genoa, and Venice grew wealthy in the process of importing silks from Antioch, cotton from Tripoli, ironwork from Beirut, glass and pottery from Tyre, and perfume from Nablus. In turn they provided the Crusaders with a constant flow of men, grain, and arms.

During the reign of Fulk of Anjou (1131-1143) the Latin Kingdom reached its zenith. The conquests of the Crusaders had been consolidated and, while the Arab population was not happy to be subject to Christians, a tolerable relationship had been established. Commerce with Europe had brought a measure of prosperity to the land.

While the Christians were consolidating their power and showing a measure of success in the Holy Land, the Muslim rulers were planning their day of reconquest. Imad ad-Din of Mosul gathered a following among the Turkish-Arab territories of Mesopotamia before approaching the Crusader cities. In 1128 he attacked Aleppo and thereby drove a wedge into Syria itself. He was unable to follow up this advantage for a decade because of the necessity of strengthening his hold on the Euphrates region. That accomplished, he returned to Syria and laid siege to the fortified stronghold of Edessa. In December, 1144, the city fell and Imad ad-Din slaughtered its Christian citizens. Fear fell upon Antioch and Jerusalem in the realization that the initiative in battle now belonged to the Muslim leaders.

In 1146 Pope Eugenius III called for a new crusade, and Bernard of Clairvaux called upon Christian Europe to return to the Holy Land in defense of Christianity there. Conrad III of Germany and Louis VII of France came forward to lead the Second Crusade and messengers went ahead to Jerusalem to herald the news that help was on the way. The results were disastrous, however. The Europeans passed as a lawless mob

through Byzantium and terrorized its citizens, so alienating them
that they offered no real assistance to their fellow Christians.
They managed to reach Damascus but there the noble mission
came to an inglorious end. Conrad left the country immediately,
and Louis followed after making a pilgrimage to Jerusalem to
see the holy places.

The Second Crusade was the last serious attempt of the
Europeans to turn back the growing tide of Muslim power.
Imad ad-Din was succeeded by his son Nur ad-Din who was as
effective on the battlefield as his father had been during the
previous decade. Nur ad-Din added territory in the regions of
Edessa and Antioch, so that by 1164 the land route from Jerusalem to Constantinople was closed. Northern Syria was firmly
in Turkish hands.

Meanwhile a Muslim prince in Egypt named Salah ad-Din,
Saladin to the Europeans, came to the fore as Islam's leading
champion. Saladin gained control of Egypt from the decadent
Fatimid dynasty and, after the death of Nur ad-Din (1174), he
gained control of Syria as well. During the decade from 1174 to
1184 he gained control of Mesopotamia from the Turkish princes.
Then, with a united Muslim world behind him he was ready to
take on the Franks.

In March of 1187 Saladin was ready to move against the
Christians. With an army of about a hundred thousand well-
armed Turks he moved southward into Galilee. The Crusaders
hastily gathered a force of about fifty thousand to protect Jerusalem. The armies met for the first time at Tiberias, but on the
second day the outnumbered Christians fell back in disorder.
The Turks then surrounded the Christians at the twin-peaked
mountain known as the Horns of Hattin. The Christians might
have fought their way out of this trap, but Saladin ordered the
dry grass of the plain fired, and thousands of Franks were
smothered in the burning grass, while others fell at the hands of
the Turks as they sought to escape. The disaster at Hattin was,
for all practical purposes, the end of Crusader power in the
Holy Land.

Acre, Caesarea, Nablus, and a score of other armed towns fell
to Saladin in a matter of weeks. Late in September, 1187,
Saladin's siege engines were erected on the west side of Jerusalem. Legend suggests that Saladin planned to take the city
by force as the Crusaders had done nearly a century before. The
Christian leader, the story goes, threatened to massacre every
Muslim in the city and to raze the Dome of the Rock (the

Christian "Temple of Solomon") unless a lenient surrender could be arranged. Whether the legend is true or not, the Christians capitulated on October 2, and Saladin's terms were relatively lenient.

The Franks were required to pay a heavy ransom whether they stayed or left the country. Most sold their houses and possessions and left, but the Syrians and the children of earlier Franko-Syrian marriages for the most part stayed, and many of them embraced Islam to avoid the heavy burden of taxation. Blond-haired, blue-eyed Arab children in the Holy Land are part of the Crusader's legacy to the East.

There could be no question that Islam was in firm control of Jerusalem. The cross above the Dome of the Rock was struck down and the rock itself was cleansed with rose water. Images of the saints and all the Christian furnishings were removed. The Dome of the Rock became one of Islam's holy places again.

Most of the Christian churches were converted into mosques or were adapted to other uses for the Islamic conquerors. Saladin's soldiers wanted to destroy the Church of the Holy Sepulchre, but he insisted on preserving it, although it was boarded up and its use was denied to the Christians. "Why," Saladin asked, "ruin and destroy the city, when the goal of their worship is the emplacement of the Cross and the Sepulchre, and not the buildings erected there? Even if they were razed to the ground, the various Christian communities would still come rushing to them! Let us imitate the Calif Omar, who, when he entered Jerusalem during the first years of Islam, preserved these buildings."

9

AFTER THE CRUSADES

The fall of Jerusalem to Saladin, a scant ninety years after the Crusaders had victoriously entered the city, produced consternation throughout Europe. So great was this second Arab victory that only Antioch, Tyre, and Tripoli of the vast Crusader holdings in the Near East remained in Christian hands. Pope Gregory VIII called for a new Crusade. A tenth of every man's income was demanded to underwrite the project, and once again the princes of Europe were called upon to settle their differences and head eastward. Frederick Barbarosa, who had fought in the Second Crusade, led his forces as far as Armenia, only to be drowned in the river Salep. Help came, however, from Richard I ("the Lionhearted") of England and Philip of France who became the heroes of the Third Crusade. The combined English and French forces took the city of Acre and a moment of triumph seemed imminent. Philip returned to Europe but Richard conducted his army southward toward Jerusalem. Fighting both the weather and the Muslim forces of Saladin, the brave Richard came to the sensible conclusion that the Europeans could not hope to permanently vanquish the people whose home was in the East. Saladin also recognized that the Christians, both European and Syrian, could not be permanently kept out of the country. Following a battle at Jaffa, in which the small Crusader force fought valiantly against Saladin's larger army, a truce was arranged. The Christians would control the seacoast between Acre and Jaffa and they would have rights of pilgrimage, free of taxes, to Jerusalem.

The idea that Muslim, Christian, and Jew could co-exist in the Holy Land was something of a revolutionary idea. While Richard's truce was soon forgotten, the precedent had been set and

Christian churches and Muslim mosques began to dot the cities of Palestine and the majority of the people of both faiths were content to accept one another.

In the years that followed, Europe continued to send Crusaders to the Muslim East, but political considerations became even more important than they had been during the earliest Crusades. Muslim leaders in Damascus vied with their co-religionists in Cairo, and each wooed the crusading Christians. In 1229 and again in 1241 Crusaders actually controlled Jerusalem for short periods. Rival factions among both Muslims and Christians were suddenly faced with a new threat when the Khwarizmian tribe of Turks pushed out from Persia into the Middle East.

The Khwarizmians were one of the peoples that suffered as a result of the Mongol invasions led by Chingiz Khan. Having been driven out of their own country, the Khwarizmians moved into Syria and Palestine. The Egyptian calif seems to have encouraged them to take Jerusalem with the idea that they would finally drive the Christians out. The result was a massacre. Christians who did not flee were slaughtered. After three years of bloodshed even the Egyptians had to turn against the Khwarizmians to stop the pillage which had spread from Christian to Muslim cities. During this time the last Crusader influence was wiped out and the Crusader strongholds were left in ruins.

Syrian Christians and Arab-Turk Muslims continued to live in the desolate Jerusalem, maintaining their holy places and hoping for better days. Another Turkish tribe — the Ottoman Turks as they were later called — fled before the Mongols and found a home in Asia Minor. For five centuries the empire they founded ruled the lands of the eastern Mediterranean. In 1453 the great Byzantine capital of Constantinople fell to the Ottomans, bringing the Eastern Roman Empire to an end. In 1517, Selim I added Egypt to his Ottoman Empire and proclaimed himself calif over the entire Muslim world. Selim's son Suleiman "the Magnificent" set about to restore the religious shrines of Islam throughout Asia Minor, Syria, and Palestine. In Jerusalem he laid out the Haram, or Temple Area, in the form in which it appears today. Still more conspicuous, the present walls of the city are those built by Suleiman.

Suleiman adopted those policies of governing the religious groups within his empire that are still practiced throughout the Middle East. Although his state was Muslim, he encouraged both Jews and Christians to take positions of responsibility.

THE DAMASCUS GATE leading into the Old City from the north. The present walls were built during the reign of Suleiman the Magnificent.

Suffering the pogroms of Europe, many Jews made their way to the Turkish Empire, where their learning, particularly in the area of medicine, was much appreciated. From the Christian communities in the Balkans, in Greece, and in Hungary, the Ottomans placed a levy — at first one out of every five young men — for military service. The troops, known as Janizaries (*Yenicheri*, "New Troops"), were an effective fighting company, and the most intelligent received special training for governmental responsibility. In this way Christians rose to become chief officers of the sultans.

While the Ottoman Empire maintained a tight hold on the political life of its people, many of the personal matters — marriage, inheritance, divorce, observance of religious law — were delegated to religious leaders of the respective communities. Jews and Christians were permitted to pursue their religious activities in comparative peace. Islam, Judaism, and Christianity were represented in Palestine, and the adherents to each looked to their own religious courts for judicial decisions in many of the activities of daily life.

A fresh threat to the peace of the Holy Land came in the person of Napoleon whose interest was politically motivated. Napoleon saw Palestine as a land bridge between Asia and

Africa, the gateway to the Middle East. In 1798 Napoleon's fleet landed at Alexandria and in the Battle of the Pyramids that followed, French arms prevailed. Although Ottoman power had been ineffective in Egypt for a generation, the sultan in Constantinople still claimed Egypt as part of his empire. The British — allies of the Ottomans against Napoleon — sent their fleet to Egypt and fought the Battle of the Nile which decimated the Napoleonic navy. Napoleon was forced to spend the winter in Egypt, and his staff gave attention to governmental reforms and archaeological study. The world of scholarship is grateful for the work of Napoleon's savants in Egypt, for it led to the discovery of the tri-lingual Rosetta stone. A French soldier, digging a trench near Rosetta (Rashid), discovered a large stone with three versions of an inscription — two forms of ancient Egyptian and one of Greek. This provided the long-sought solution to the problem of deciphering the hieroglyphic writing of ancient Egypt. Scholars used the Greek version of the inscription as the key and eventually came to read the Egyptian texts. The science of Egyptology was thus born. Napoleon's military defeat by the British meant that the Rosetta Stone went to the British Museum rather than the Louvre, but it was a Frenchman, Champollion, who first deciphered the hieroglyphs.

The Ottoman forces moved by land and sea against Napoleon in 1799. After the disastrous Battle of the Nile, Napoleon was in no position to launch a naval expedition against the sultan, so he marched his armies into Palestine. On March 6 he took Jaffa, then marched on to Acre. The British navy prevented the French from landing their siege guns, and Napoleon had to retreat. He made his way back to Egypt and stayed there until August, when he returned to Paris.

The sultan claimed power over Egypt once more and confirmed one of his able generals, Muhammad Ali, as viceroy in Egypt with the title of pasha. Muhammad Ali continued the reforms which Napoleon had instituted. In 1831 he revolted against the sultan, declaring his independence. With his son Ibrahim, Muhammad Ali ruled both Egypt and the Holy Land, and they dreamed of an empire that would absorb all of the Ottoman territories. The European powers of Britain, France, and Russia, while no admirers of the Ottomans, feared the results of Ali's ambition, and backed the sultan. Egypt and Palestine were thus restored to the Ottomans.

During the eight years that Muhammad Ali had controlled the Holy Land he opened the country to Western travelers and provided for their protection, a policy which was continued by the Ottomans. The telegraph and improved roads eased the burden of the pilgrim and the scholar. The European powers accepted the responsibility for protecting travelers, worshipers, and holy places. The Russians took the responsibility for the Greek Orthodox, the French and Austrians for the Roman Catholics, and the British and Prussians for the Protestants. The British consuls were instructed to concern themselves with the rights of Jewish residents and travelers.

The result of this system of "protection" was the practical exemption of foreigners from Turkish jurisdiction. Each consulate maintained its own guard, its own courts, and its own post office. The Russian mission built a compound of hospices around a Russian cathedral. The Germans built a German colony in the valley of Rephaim and, after the state visit of Kaiser Wilhelm II they erected the Church of the Dormition on Mt. Zion and the Victoria-Augusta Hospital on Mt. Scopus. The French built the first railroad from the coast to Jerusalem in the 1880's and this provided safe and rapid transportation. In the 1860's, 1870's and 1880's, competent scholars began to undertake the scientific study of the Holy Land. The British Ordnance Survey produced the first exact plan of Jerusalem, and scholars from the United States, Britain, and France began their pioneer work.

During the nineteenth century the Jewish population of Jerusalem increased rapidly. In 1827 there were but 1,500 Jews in the city, but by 1873 the Jewish population had risen to 10,600. They formed a majority of the population for the first time since the destruction of Jerusalem by the armies of Titus in A.D. 70. By 1910, 50,000 of the 68,000 inhabitants of Jerusalem were Jews.

In 1837 the wealthy Jewish banker and philanthropist, Sir Moses Montefiore, visited the Holy Land. His concern over the plight of his co-religionists there sparked those developments which would ultimately become Zionism and the State of Israel. The Jews of Palestine were living on alms provided by Jews of other lands who wished to maintain a group of pious scholars studying the Torah (Law) in the sacred precincts of Jerusalem. Fights between landowners and bedouin tribes had resulted in the destruction of thousands of acres of cultivated soil with the result that the Jews of Palestine had little hope of ever becoming self-sufficient. Montefiore tried to buy or rent land on which to settle Jewish families. His efforts were largely unsuccessful, but in 1854 he persuaded the Ottoman sultan to sell him land in the vicinity of Safad on which to settle fifty-four Jewish families.

The French Rothschilds undertook similar projects. Before the end of the century persecuted Jews of eastern Europe were looking for new homes. Most fled west, but some made their way to the Holy Land.

The earliest Jewish settlers from Europe faced unforeseen difficulties. They had no training in agriculture, and yet they tried to farm land that had been neglected for centuries. Their presence was resented by the local Arab population, and the Ottoman government banned ownership of land by the Jews. Ultimately the Rothschild family undertook their support singlehandedly.

Theodor Herzl, a young Austrian journalist who knew nothing of the struggles of Jews in Palestine, was horrified at the anti-Semitism which revealed itself in the Dreyfus affair. He decided to do something about it, and through his publications and his organizing ability he became the father of modern Zionism. The concept of Palestine as a national homeland for the Jews was but an idea in the minds of idealistic Zionists until World War I when it became British policy. The Balfour Declaration stated:

> His Majesty's Government view with favor the establishment in Palestine of a national home for the Jewish people, and will use their best endeavours to facilitate the achievement of this object, it being clearly understood that nothing shall be done which may prejudice the civil and religious rights of existing non-Jewish communities in Palestine or the rights and political status enjoyed by Jews in any other country.

The Balfour Declaration had been made during war, when military considerations were of paramount importance. Chaim Weizmann, a Russian-born Jewish chemist on the staff of the University of Manchester, had played an important part in the development of the explosive TNT. Arthur James Balfour and the British cabinet were sympathetic with Weizmann's Zionism, and rewarded him with the Balfour Declaration.

The Jews, however, were not the only people to be considered in Palestine. The Declaration itself acknowledged that "non-Jewish communities" might have rights which would have to be guarded. Young Arab leaders were anxious to throw off the Ottoman yoke and make Palestine an Arab state. Espousing the cause of Arab nationalism was a young British officer, T. E. Lawrence, "Lawrence of Arabia," who almost miraculously welded together the Arab tribes with the promise of freedom.

THE SHRINE OF THE SCROLLS on the campus of Hebrew University. The white cupola and the black basalt wall represent the battle between the Sons of Light and the Sons of Darkness described in the Qumran War Scroll, one of the scrolls preserved in the shrine. Courtesy, Israel Information Services

THE DOME OF THE SHRINE, with the cylinder containing the Book of Isaiah from Qumran, Cave I. Courtesy, Israel Information Services

WRITING TABLES from Qumran. Courtesy, Archaeological Museum, Jerusalem

EXHIBIT OF DEAD SEA SCROLLS from the shrine at Hebrew University.
Courtesy, Israel Information Services

Within a matter of months after the Balfour Declaration, a second British statement was made:

> The end that France and Great Britain have in pursuing in the East the war unloosed by German ambition is the complete and definite freeing of the peoples so long oppressed by the Turks and the establishment of national governments and administrations deriving their authority from the free choice of the indigenous populations.

Taking advantage of Lawrence's desert revolt, the British entered Palestine from Egypt in the fall of 1917. After a campaign of but six weeks, Viscount Allenby entered Jerusalem in the name of the British crown and the allied forces. A Christian power again controlled the Holy City, but no changes in its political or religious life were contemplated. Allenby pledged himself to maintain the status quo. Early in 1919 Allenby sent for Chaim Weizmann, the Zionist leader, and the Emir Feisal, leader of the Arab nationalists. The attempt to fuse the two communities was to prove more than Britain could handle.

At the close of World War I the newly-organized League of Nations confirmed Palestine as a British-mandated territory and the British proceeded to implement their announced policy. The Jewish population of Jerusalem doubled so that by 1946 there were 102,000 Jews in the city of 165,000. Industries were introduced and Jerusalem became the headquarters of the Jewish Agency and of the Mandatory Central Government. In 1925 the Hebrew University was opened on Mount Scopus, east of the city. A medical center was built nearby. American philanthropy provided the Palestine Archaeological Museum, and the YMCA building which still dominates the skyline of Jerusalem. The British built a new post office and a residence for the High Commissioner. Suburbs developed west of the Old City to accommodate the influx of Jewish immigrants.

The rapid increase in Jewish population understandably disturbed the Arabs. The Arab leader, or Grand Mufti, of Jerusalem, Haj Amin el-Husseini, was bitterly anti-Jewish, and he adopted a hard line against Zionist hopes. In 1922, 1929, and from 1936 to 1939 the streets of Jerusalem were the scene of bloody riots. The mandatory forces were unable to keep the peace in Jerusalem, and the British Foreign Office reversed its World War I policy and strictly limited Jewish immigration.

The internal struggles of Palestine were temporarily suspended during World War II as the Jews backed Britain in its

war against Hitler. Resentments against the British grew, however, as Jewish refugees from Europe were denied admission to
the Holy Land. Some managed to enter the country illegally,
and some perished in the Mediterranean making the attempt.
To the Jews of Palestine, the British appeared to be the allies of
the Arabs in keeping Jews out of the country. Jewish terrorist
organizations arose to take the law into their own hands, and
bloodshed continued.

The mandate was clearly a failure and the British served
notice to the United Nations that they intended to leave the
country. Compromise solutions to the "Palestine problem" were
unacceptable to either side. In 1947 the problem was presented
to the United Nations General Assembly, and that body worked
out a division of the country between the two rival groups. Parts
of the country where Jews were in the majority were assigned
to them, and the Arabs were to govern the areas where they
were in the majority. Economically and politically the division
presented insuperable problems, but to the U.N. it seemed the
only feasible solution. The British announced that they would
leave the country on May 15, 1948. Conditions were so tense
that the U.N. was unable to establish a governing committee in
Jerusalem. On the afternoon of May 14 the Jewish National
Council met informally in Tel Aviv. David Ben-Gurion announced the establishment of the state of Israel just eight hours
before the British mandatory government was due to end.

With the withdrawal of the British, Jew and Arab faced one
another in bitter warfare. An initial Jewish advance into the Old
City was repulsed by the Arab Legion. The old Jewish Quarter
had to be abandoned. The Jews were able to defend the western
suburbs, known as the New City, at great cost. The city was
cut off from the thriving Jewish settlements along the coastal
plain by a series of Arab villages along the connecting road.
The wrecks of Jewish convoys sent to relieve Jerusalem are still
beside the road, left there by Israelis to commemorate the
fighting. Shortly before the First Armistice of June, 1948, a new
road circumventing the Arab positions at Latrun was opened to
the plain. This so-called "Burma Road" made it possible for Jews
to get fresh supplies of food and ammunition into Jerusalem.

Jews and Arabs both agreed to a truce of one month to allow
the U.N. mediator, Count Bernadotte of Sweden, to work out
terms of a permanent peace. During the third week of the truce,
Bernadotte issued his report which called for the Jews to leave
the whole of Jerusalem and to turn the city over to Abdullah of

THE ECCE HOMO ARCH at the beginning of the Via Dolorosa. Christian pilgrims commemorate the events leading up to the crucifixion of Christ at the "stations of the cross" along this road which leads to the Church of the Holy Sepulchre.

Transjordan. The earlier partition plan had called for the internationalization of Jerusalem under the U.N. — a plan unacceptable to Jew and Arab alike. This plan antagonized the Jews, and Bernadotte himself was subsequently murdered by Jewish extremists.

The truce was broken as Jew and Arab faced one another again. Both groups had used the period of the truce to rearm, and when hostilities began a second time on July 2, the Jews

felt confident that they could recapture the Old City. Under
U.N. auspices a second truce was called and the fighting ended
officially on July 18.

The armistice that followed was an uneasy one. On December 10, 1948, the United Nations acknowledged the existence of the State of Israel. The borders at the cessation of
hostilities were accepted as Israel's de facto boundary. Ralph
Bunche, Count Bernadotte's successor, negotiated a series of
treaties between Israel and the Arab states to guarantee peace
behind the existing frontiers.

After 1948 Jerusalem was a divided city. The Old City
and the area north of it were part of the Hashemite Kingdom of
Jordan, the successor state to the former Transjordan. The
Palestine Archaeological Museum and the American School of
Oriental Research were in the Jordanian sector of Jerusalem. The
original campus of the Hebrew University-Hadassah Hospital on
Mount Scopus was considered Israeli territory, but it was en-
tirely surrounded by Jordan and free access was denied to the
Jews. The only contact was through the U.N.

Jordanian Jerusalem continued to be a major tourist attraction.
Within the Old City Christians still walked the Via Dolorosa to
the Church of the Holy Sepulchre, performing the Stations of the
Cross each Friday afternoon. Many Christians as well as Muslims visited the Haram, or Temple area, to see the Dome of the
Rock, the El-Aksa Mosque and the complex of Muslim structures
that mark sites going back to Old Testament times. No Jew was
allowed to go to the old Wailing Wall, however, for Jordan and
Israel maintained no diplomatic ties. To the Jordanian, Israel
did not exist. It was merely "Jewish occupied Palestine."

To the old hospices and religious centers were added new
hotels to accommodate the tourist who enjoys a bit of luxury.
Latest of these was the Jerusalem Intercontinental Hotel on the
Mount of Olives, overlooking the Old City.

Israeli Jerusalem has enjoyed phenomenal growth since 1948.
The religious life of the city found its focus in a new build-
ing with the impressive title, Hechal Schlomo — "Temple of
Solomon" — actually named for Solomon Wolfson of Great Brit-
ain, who contributed a substantial part of the funds for the
building. On a long, narrow ridge called Givat Ram, a new
campus has been built for the Hebrew University, with the
Israeli National Museum on a nearby hilltop. Five miles west of
Jerusalem is the new thirty-million-dollar Hadassah Medical
Center.

THE NEW ISRAEL MUSEUM in Jerusalem, with the Judean hills in the background. Courtesy, Israel Information Services

In June of 1967, after Gamal Abdel Nasser closed the Gulf of Aqaba to Israeli shipping and the Arab world rallied to his side. Israel pushed southward and westward to seize the Sinai Peninsula, and eastward as far as the Jordan River. This brought the Old City of Jerusalem into Israeli hands and made it possible for the Jews to visit the holy places, particularly the "Wailing Wall," for the first time since 1948.

While regretting the tragedies of Jerusalem's long history, the visitor is encouraged to see progress in Jerusalem today. While recognizing the animosities which divide peoples here, as elsewhere, he seeks to remember the Psalmist's plea: "Pray for the peace of Jerusalem: they shall prosper that love thee."

BIBLIOGRAPHY

JERUSALEM

Avi-Yonah, Michael, *Jerusalem* (New York: 1960).
  The Madaba Mosaic Map (Jerusalem, Israel: 1954).
  Sepher Yerushalaim ("The Book of Jerusalem" — in Hebrew).
    (Jerusalem and Tel Aviv, 1956).

Caldecott, W. Shaw, *The Second Temple in Jerusalem* (London: 1908).

Join-Lambert, Michel, *Jerusalem* (London: 1958).

Laffont, Robert, ed., *Histoire de Jerusalem* (Paris: 1965).

Joseph, Dov, *The Faithful City* (New York: 1960).

Leconte, Rene, *Jerusalem* (Paris: 1954).

Merrill, Selah, *Ancient Jerusalem* (New York: 1908).

Simons, J., *Jerusalem in the Old Testament* (Leiden: 1952).

Smith, George Adam, *Jerusalem from the Earliest Times to A.D. 70* (London: 1907-08).

Vincent, L. H. and Steve, A. M., *Jerusalem de l' Ancien Testament* (Paris: 1954-56).

Williams, Albert N., *The Holy City* (New York: 1954).

Wilson, R. E., Warren, R. E. and others, *The Discovery of Jerusalem* (New York: 1871).

THE HOLY LAND

Aharoni, Yohanan, *The Land of the Bible* (London: 1966).

Avi-Yonah, Michael, *The Holy Land from the Persian to the Arab Conquest* (Grand Rapids: 1966).

Baly, Denis, *The Geography of the Bible* (New York: 1957).

Bright, John, *A History of Israel* (Philadelphia: 1959).

Noth, Martin, *The Old Testament World* (London: 1966).

Pfeiffer, Charles, *Baker's Bible Atlas* (Grand Rapids: 1961).

Thomson, W. M., *The Land and the Book* (New York: 1880-1885).

Vilnay, Zev, *The Holy Land in Old Prints and Maps* Jerusalem: 1963).

Smith, George Adam, *The Historical Geography of the Holy Land* (New York: 1966).

INDEX

91